# Memories of Pope Pius X

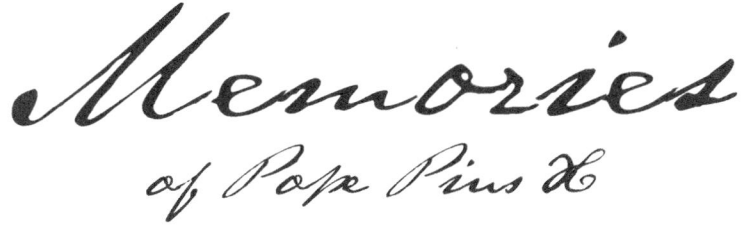

# Memories of Pope Pius X

Cardinal Merry del Val

*Forewords by*

CARDINAL HINSLEY
ARCHBISHOP OF WESTMINSTER

*and*

CARDINAL HAYES
LATE ARCHBISHOP OF NEW YORK

PO Box 217 | Saint Marys, KS 66536

First published 1939
Reprinted by The Newman Press 1951

NIHIL OBSTAT :
Ernestus Messenger, Ph.D.,
*Censor deputatus.*

IMPRIMATUR :
E. Morrogh Bernard,
*Vic. Gen.*

Westmonasterii,
*die 21a Junii 1939.*

# ANGELUS PRESS
PO Box 217
Saint Marys, Kansas 66536
Phone (816) 753-3150
Fax (816) 753-3557
Order Line 1-800-966-7337
**www.angeluspress.org**

ISBN: 978-1-68529-055-9
Angelus Press Edition–November 2023

# CONTENTS

| | |
|---|---|
| Foreword by H.E. Cardinal Hinsley | 1 |
| Foreword by H.E. Cardinal Hayes | 3 |
| Editor's Note | 11 |
| Introductory | 13 |
| I. My First Meeting with H.E. Cardinal Sarto | 15 |
| II. My First Audience with Pius X | 20 |
| III. Pius X and His First Reception of the Diplomatic Corps | 26 |
| IV. Impressions of Statesmen Concerning Pius X | 32 |
| V. My Nomination as Cardinal Secretary of State | 36 |
| VI. Pius X and the Great War | 42 |
| VII. Characteristics of Pius X | 48 |
| VIII. His Learning and Eloquence | 67 |

|      |                          |     |
| ---: | ------------------------ | --: |
| IX.  | Pius X and the Arts      | 80  |
| X.   | Pius X and Music         | 91  |
| XI.  | His Charity              | 98  |
| XII. | The New Code of Canon Law | 104 |
| XIII.| His Humility             | 111 |
| XIV. | Last Illness and Death   | 123 |
| XV.  | His Relatives            | 134 |

# FOREWORD
BY
CARDINAL HINSLEY
*Archbishop of Westminster*

In simple sincerity a man of God tells of his intimate knowledge of another man of God, as St. Bonaventure wrote of St. Francis of Assisi. The greatness of both as men of high estate, spiritual and temporal, is hidden in the simplicity of the one and of the other. A Secretary of State looks at the Vicar of Christ through the eyes of his admiring affection for his saintly master. Cardinal Merry del Val serves and imitates Pius X.

This little book of personal memories will charm and attract all who read it. The devotion and love of the aristocratic secretary reflect the qualities of the humble peasant who was raised to the highest dignity on earth; the two became united in the service and following of their Divine Master.

Outwardly they were contrasted: their inward spirit became more and more identified. The simple epitaph on the tomb of Cardinal

Merry del Val in the Crypt of St. Peter's explains the bond of their supernatural intimacy:

*Da mihi animas coetera tolle.*[1]

---

[1] Give me souls and take everything else.

# FOREWORD
BY
CARDINAL HAYES
*Late Archbishop of New York*

THE paternal and saintly figure of Pope Pius X, of blessed memory, looks out appealingly from these pages as if his soul would continue his remarkable influence on the children of men. No pen other than that of his devoted Secretary of State, the late lamented Cardinal Merry del Val, could present with such intimate knowledge the captivating personality of him who as Vicar of Christ left so ineffaceable an impression on his time.

The Pontiff was above all a supreme pastor of souls. His entire being breathed a burning zeal and all-consuming love of the universal flock committed to his care by Christ. Especially was he devoted to children at the Communion Table and in the catechism class. This was impressively illustrated in the Decree on Frequent Communion, and Communion to children of tender age. His memory will remain endeared to the little ones of our day as well as of centuries yet unborn. The Chief Shepherd of Christendom boldly changed a fixed discipline of the Church when he opened the Tabernacle to uncover the Ciborium that Christ's innocent children might come unto Him in the Eucharist and partake of the Bread of Angels.

So absorbed was His Holiness in the exercise of the pastoral office that his humility, simplicity, and kindliness became dominant in a radiant splendour which somewhat obscured other stirring, outstanding endowments of his wonderful character that were less present to the popular mind.

In a recent life of Cardinal Merry del Val by Monsignor Cenci, one of the photographs of Pius X represents the Pontiff at his desk. It is significant that alongside the Crucifix is seen a statue of St. John Baptist Vianney, Curé d'Ars, the simple parish priest who evidently was a beloved patron of the Holy Father. Rather one might look for the image of a great apostle, an outstanding doctor of the Church, or some illustrious pontiff.

It may be remarked here that the yearning ambition of Cardinal Merry del Val was not to serve in a diplomatic career or exalted office in the Church. His ardent prayer was that God would give him souls and cast his life as parish priest among the poor. This spirit with regard to the pastoral ministry was one that made the Pope and his secretary closely akin.

The affectionate attachment of Pius X to his gifted secretary sets a notable value on the short sketches of the Holy Father herein written by the Cardinal, who proved to be to the Pontiff a most devoted son, an indefatigable servant, and an eminently understanding co-worker. Of the secretary, the Vicar of Christ did say that he 'did not know how to thank God sufficiently for the priceless gift of his co-labourer.'

The Cardinal within the covers of this small volume unveils a portrait of Pius X that more completely presents the full figure of the Pontiff than the prevalent idea of him held by the faithful.

The Pope had a very large, broad and comprehensive ideal of the pastoral office of the Vicar of Christ. His apostolic spirit endowed him with a searching vision that enabled him to see, understand and appreciate the world over which he ruled, at its proper estimate with regard to faith and morals. His mind was keenly alert to detect error in its first manifestation, and his heart was courageous to act promptly. Truly, Pius was a vigilant watchman in the citadel of Divine Truth. His vigorous and successful attack on Modernism bears testimony to this historic fact.

A rare quality of exalted leadership was inborn in Pius X as his remarkable pontificate reveals. His Holiness would have manifested in civil government a most impressive statesmanship had he been called to a secular career. He made an abiding, monumental contribution to ecclesiastical legislation in the codification of canon law. It is not easily realized that the present compact volume, containing the body of law for the Latin Church, is a practical epitome of centuries of legislative action of popes, councils and synods, presented with such marvellous clarity of exposition and simplicity of arrangement that the Code is made available for the humblest parish priest. This work alone is sufficient to place the Pontiff among the great popes of history.

Pius X was ever occupied with a variety of abiding interests and practices of Holy Church because of an all-consuming zeal. He showed exceptional solicitude for higher biblical studies to offset the destructive criticism of Sacred Scripture by scholars outside the faith. With regard to Divine Worship, he reformed the Roman Breviary and restored to the Liturgy the venerable sacred chant of the Church.

Rare was the cultural side of the Pontiff. 'He loved beautiful things.' Architecture, painting, music and even the art of making Venetian lace appealed to his delicate sense of beauty.

The Cardinal's testimony corroborates what we know from many other sources of the inspiring and lasting impression Pius made in his public utterances and during liturgical functions. No uncommon occurrence was it that those privileged to see or hear him were moved to their very soul by the manifest all-embracing affection of the Universal Father of Christendom, the humility and simplicity of the common shepherd of the faithful the world over, and the unction of his apostolic heart stirred by the Holy Spirit. I personally in audience witnessed a prominent American official, a non-Catholic, in tears as he knelt for the blessing of the Holy Father. An aura of spiritual majesty surrounded this great, noble, but humble Vicar of Christ. To the majesty of this humility the Cardinal beautifully calls attention by stating that it had become to Pius a second nature. '*Ubi humilitas, ibi majestas.*' (St. Augustine)

The spirit of poverty was closely united in the Pontiff with humility and simplicity. The climax of the Cardinal's tribute herein set forth, it seems to me, is the reference to the Last Will and Testament of Pius, who wrote: 'Born poor, having lived poor, and certain to die poor.'

An American gentleman asked the Cardinal on one occasion the reason of the apparent delay with regard to the beatification of Pius X, since by almost universal acclaim among the faithful he was held to be a saint. Moreover, the canonization of the Little Flower within a comparatively short period was cited to justify a speedy process for the holy Pontiff. His Eminence replied that it was not difficult to canonize a child entering Carmel at a tender age and observing cloister for the rest of her life, but it was no easy matter for the Church to raise to sainthood one who had lived to his eightieth year. His long life, holy though it was, demands a searching scrutiny of every thought, word and deed over three-quarters of a century. The fact that as Vicar of Christ he had the burden of terrifying responsibilities makes the investigation all the more imperative.

May the year of the Lord in the Providence of God soon arrive that will give glory to God in the highest and joy unbounded to the faithful on earth by reason of the canonization of Pope Pius X!

This brief review of the Cardinal's tribute to the Pontiff may be happily concluded by referring to His Eminence's own tender piety and saintliness of life. To those privileged to observe the Cardinal closely, the very humility of Pius was mirrored in his secretary. The exalted office the latter occupied with such rare distinction, served to emphasize the lowliness of his devout soul with regard to personal evaluation of the invaluable service he rendered the Church.

Is it too presumptuous to pray and hope that the beloved secretary of Pope Pius X may have been inspired so spiritually under the influence of Christ's Vicar that one day not far distant another St. Raphael may be raised to the Altars of the Church!

# EDITOR'S NOTE[1]

The publication of the *Memories of Pope Pius X* in this year, the tenth anniversary of the death of H.E. Cardinal Merry del Val, is due to the kindness of Cardinal Nicola Canali, who was the close friend of the saintly Cardinal for thirty years, and was named as his executor in his will. He carefully treasured all the manuscripts of the dead Cardinal, among them these *Memories*. In response to many requests from distinguished admirers of Cardinal Merry del Val in England and America he has now given his kind permission for their publication.

Our thanks are also due to H.E. Cardinal Hinsley for the foreword to this little volume. His friendship with Cardinal Merry del Val dates from his seminary days at Ushaw, and continued until the day of the Cardinal's death. At that time Cardinal Merry del Val was Cardinal protector of the Venerable English

---

[1] Written in 1939, when *Memories of Pope Pius X* was first published.

College, Rome, of which Monsignor Hinsley was Rector.

The foreword of H.E. Cardinal Hayes was written some time before his death for a future American edition of the *Memories*. It is added here because of its great interest. The venerated Cardinal Archbishop of New York, the 'Cardinal of Charity' to his American children, testifies to his devotion to the Pope of charity, Pius X, and to that other 'Cardinal of Charity,' his great namesake, Raphael Cardinal Merry del Val.

The editor is responsible for the English translation of the article from the *Revue Pratique d'Apologétique* on page 51 and of the extract from the *Lettre Pastorale* of Cardinal Mercier on page 54.

J. P. C. A.

# INTRODUCTORY

In 1905 Monsignor Marchesan published a life of His Holiness Pius X, extending from his birth and early years up to the time of his election as Sovereign Pontiff.[1] With abundant material at his disposal, and in constant touch with all those who had known Giuseppe Sarto from his youth and later on when he became a priest, Bishop of Mantua and Cardinal Patriarch of Venice, Monsignor Marchesan has compiled a remarkable history which, I fancy, it will be difficult to surpass in accuracy and completeness. Since then, in 1918, F. A. Forbes has given us a brief life of Pius X, written with the ability and charm which distinguish the author of *The Standard-bearers of the Faith*.[2]

A real history of the pontificate of the late Holy Father has still to appear and I presume that most people will agree that it is too early

---

[1] *Papa Pio X nella sua Vita e nella sua Parola. Studio storico del suo vecchio allievo, il sac.* Dott. Angelo Marchesan. Benziger, Einsiedeln, 1905.
[2] *Life of Pius X*, by F. A. Forbes. Burns, Oates & Washbourne Ltd., London, 1918.

in the day and hardly possible to attempt the task at present.

The following sketches, for they do not claim to be more than that, may be of interest to those, and they are many, who venerate the memory of the great and saintly Pontiff. I have been persuaded to publish them by friends who have assured me that I can do so without indiscretion. They narrate simple facts that I am able to vouch for, and I have carefully refrained from going beyond the limits of personal reminiscences.

# MEMORIES OF POPE PIUS X

I

## MY FIRST MEETING WITH H.E. CARDINAL SARTO

STRANGE it may seem, but it is nevertheless a fact, that I had not met His Eminence Cardinal Sarto before the end of July, 1903, when the Sacred College assembled in Conclave after the death of His Holiness Pope Leo XIII. I knew every other cardinal present then in Rome, by sight at all events, and I could recognize each one. During the eight years I had spent in the Vatican in attendance on Leo XIII, I had frequent occasions of approaching nearly all the members of the Sacred College, but somehow or other I had always missed Cardinal Sarto. It was on Monday, August 3, 1903, that I enjoyed the privilege of speaking to him for the first time.

The day before had witnessed the odious 'veto' raised by Austrian politicians against Cardinal Rampolla. It is my certain conviction that the latter would have never been elected in any case, for the majority of the electors was firmly intent upon choosing some other candidate. But he ran a good chance of obtaining the necessary votes precisely when the great indignation aroused by the act of Cardinal Puszyna in the name of the Emperor of Austria produced a reaction of sentiment and an impulse to protest at any cost in defence of the liberty of the Conclave and of the rights of Holy Church.

The Cardinal Dean, Oreglia di Santo Stefano, on the morning of Monday, August 3, immediately after the first session in the Sistine Chapel, spoke to me very seriously and at length of his increasing anxiety regarding the election. There seemed to be no chance, he said, of a prompt issue if Cardinal Sarto, whose votes had steadily increased, continued in his attitude of resistance and were absolutely to refuse his acceptance of the Papacy. His Eminence felt bound in conscience not to allow things to drag on indefinitely and he therefore

# MY FIRST MEETING

bid me wait upon Cardinal Sarto and convey the following message.

I was to ask him in the name of the Cardinal Dean whether he persisted in his opposition to his election and whether he wished and authorized His Eminence to make a final and public declaration to that effect before the assembled Conclave, during the afternoon meeting; if so the Cardinal Dean would call upon his colleagues to consider the advisability of selecting some other candidate.

Accordingly I went in quest of Cardinal Sarto. I was informed that he was not in his room and that probably I should find him in the Cappella Paolina, whither I hastened to carry out my orders.

It must have been about midday when I stepped into the dark and silent chapel. The lamp before the Blessed Sacrament burned brightly and there were candles lighted high above the altar, on either side of the picture of our Lady of Good Counsel. I noticed a cardinal kneeling on the marble floor in prayer before the tabernacle, at some distance from the communion rail, his head in his hands, with his elbows resting on one of the low wooden benches, and I do not recall the presence of anybody else in the chapel at that moment. It was Cardinal Sarto. I knelt down beside him and addressing him in a whisper I secured his attention and delivered my message.

His Eminence raised his head and slowly turned his face towards me as he listened to the question I laid before him. Tears were streaming from his eyes and I almost held my breath awaiting his reply. '*Si, si, Monsignore,*' he gently answered, '*dica al Cardinale che mi faccia questa carità.*' (Yes, yes, Monsignor, tell the Cardinal to do me this act of charity.) He seemed to be echoing the words of his Divine Master in Gethsemani: '*Transeat a me calix iste.*' The 'fiat' was still to come. The only words that I found strength to utter in reply and which rose to my lips as if dictated by another, were: '*Eminenza, si faccia coraggio, il Signore l'aiuterà.*' (Eminence, take courage, our Lord will help you). The Cardinal looked fixedly at me with that deep gaze of his which I learnt to know so well; '*Grazie, grazie,*' he repeated, and that was all he said.

Once more he buried his face in his hands to resume his prayer and I left him. Never shall I forget the impression produced upon me by this first meeting and by the sight of such intense anguish. It was the first occasion on which I had come in contact with His Eminence and I felt that I had been in the presence of a saint.

A few hours later and before the Dean could carry out his request, Cardinal Sarto gave way in presence of the urgent and persistent appeals made to him by many members of the Sacred College to desist in his opposition, and after the evening session it was manifest to all that he would be elected on the morrow by a large majority.

## II

## MY FIRST AUDIENCE WITH PIUS X

THE Conclave was over. After paying homage to the newly elected Pontiff according to the established ceremonial, the Cardinals had left the Vatican to return to their residences in various parts of the city, and during the last hours of that memorable day I sat at my table in the 'Sala Borgia,' sorting papers and despatching urgent business which it was incumbent upon me to finish before going home.

When the Pope was elected that morning of August 4, I had accompanied him from his place in the Sistine Chapel to a little room on the gospel side of the altar, where he donned the white cassock and where I had the privilege of placing the white *zucchetto* on his head. He then proceeded to take his place on the chair in front of the high altar, and the Cardinals went up in turn to bow in obeisance to the newly elected Pope in the customary way. In the interval the senior cardinal deacon, Cardinal Macchi, had left the Sistine Chapel to go

## MY FIRST AUDIENCE WITH PIUS X       21

and proclaim the election of His Holiness from the balcony overlooking the great Piazza of St. Peter.

Immediately afterwards it is usual for the Pope to give his first solemn blessing *urbi et orbi*, and the Master of Ceremonies, Mgr Riggi, asked him whether he intended doing so from the loggia within the Basilica or from the one outside facing the city. Whereupon the Holy Father turned to me and inquired what the opinion was in that respect of the Sacred College. By order of the Cardinal Dean, to whom I communicated the Pope's question, I informed His Holiness that the College of Cardinals had discussed the matter before the Conclave in a meeting at which he had not been present, and whilst expressing the view that the Papal Blessing should be given within the precincts of the Basilica, following in this the example of Leo XIII, they did not wish to curtail His Holiness' freedom and left the decision to him. 'I shall be guided by the judgement of the Sacred College,' was the Pope's answer. Upon my asking him whether he wished to proceed at once to St. Peter's for that purpose or would prefer to leave it for later on in the day, he replied that it was indifferent to him and that he would do whatever appeared most suitable. I ventured to express the opinion that perhaps it would be better not to put off the ceremony and he acted accordingly.

When the blessing was over the Holy Father announced his intention of paying a visit to the aged Cardinal Herrero who, owing to illness, had not been able to assist at the election, and we accompanied His Holiness to the Cardinal's room on the way to his own apartment.

But it was not until the evening that I saw him privately and, as I then thought, to take leave. For my task as Secretary to the Sacred College in Conclave had come to an end and there only remained my last duty that night of presenting for the Pope's signature the letters addressed to the Sovereigns and heads of States to announce officially his election. I went up to his private room on the third floor, the one he had occupied during the Conclave, as the clock in the court of St. Damasus struck half-past eight, and I found the Holy Father sitting

## MY FIRST AUDIENCE WITH PIUS X

at his table reading his Breviary. I thoroughly realized how weary he must have been after that long and eventful day and I was loath to trouble him. He welcomed me with a smile and when I knelt to kiss his hand I begged him to excuse my adding to his fatigue. I was well aware, I said, how tired he must be feeling, nor should I have ventured to intrude except for the necessity of despatching these official letters without delay. '*Ma si, si, Monsignore,*' he replied in his gentle voice, '*e Lei forse non è stanco? Ho veduto quanto ha fatigato in questi giorni.*' (Why yes, yes, Monsignor: and are you not tired? I have seen how much you have worked during these days.) This unexpected answer revealed to me a characteristic feature of his which I often noticed in after years. It seemed incredible, especially in such overwhelming circumstances, that the Holy Father should so forget himself and stop to contrast his position and fatigue with mine, all the more so that I had only done what others would have done under similar conditions. But this was precisely one of the most attractive sides of his nature; he constantly thought of others, very rarely or at all of himself.

He then asked me to show him how he should sign, and on a slip of paper before him he wrote out a sample of his first signature as Pope: Pius P.P. X. When he had passed all the letters I gathered them up and begged for his blessing, for I was about to return home to my little community at the Accademia Ecclesiastica. The Holy Father made a slight gesture of surprise, apparently startled by my few words, and resting his hand on my shoulder, he said almost reproachfully: 'Monsignor, do you want to abandon me? No, no, stay, stay. I have decided nothing yet. I don't know what I shall do. For the present I have no one. Remain with me as Pro-Secretary of State: later we will see.' How could I withstand an appeal of such tenderness coming from the Vicar of Christ? I could but bow to what appeared to be almost an invitation from our Lord Himself. His Holiness bid me take courage and blessed me, adding that he would expect to see me the next morning.

Such was my first private interview with Pius X on the day of his election and the first

## MY FIRST AUDIENCE WITH PIUS X

of those daily audiences which I was privileged to enjoy for eleven years.

On returning to my room I met Monsignor Della Chiesa, who was particularly eager to see the Pope's signature and pointed out its resemblance to that of Pius IX. How far he must have been then from imagining that the next Pontiff to sign similar documents would be himself as Benedict XV!

## III

## PIUS X AND HIS FIRST RECEPTION OF THE DIPLOMATIC CORPS

ALMOST immediately after his election the Holy Father had to receive the Diplomatic Corps, and the senior member or Dean, Monsieur d'Antas, the Portuguese Ambassador, applied for the audience. In view of the excessive heat, in order to spare His Holiness unnecessary fatigue and also to meet the convenience of the Envoys who were anxious to leave Rome for their usual holiday, it was decided to hold a general reception. Monsieur d'Antas undertook to read a short address on behalf of his colleagues, offering homage to His Holiness in the name of their respective Sovereigns and Governments. The audience was fixed accordingly for August 6.

On that morning at eleven o'clock the Ambassadors and Ministers arrived at the Vatican in full uniform, accompanied by their staffs of secretaries and attachés. One of the latter confided to me later that as they ascended the great staircase in groups, several of them expressed the curiosity they felt regarding the manner in which the new Pontiff was likely to meet them. The undertaking would prove an ordeal for him, no doubt, they said; he would be embarrassed, unaccustomed as he must be to the display of a court ceremony; unlike his illustrious predecessor Leo XIII, this new Pontiff was of humble birth and reports had described him as pre-eminently a country priest. This forecast reminded me of the words of Nathanael: 'Can any thing of good come from Nazareth? Philip saith to him: Come and see.'

I was not present at the reception, for I had no place there; and I was at work in the 'Sala Borgia' when my chaplain came to inform me that the Diplomatic Corps intended calling on me as the Pro-Secretary of State immediately after the audience with His Holiness. The vast Borgia rooms afforded ample facilities for even a much larger gathering, and I quickly prepared to welcome my visitors. They all arrived shortly afterwards in brilliant array. The Envoys sat round in a semi-circle and their secretaries stood behind them.

After the first words of mutual greeting there followed a silence and I noticed that they all looked somewhat grave. Conversation drifted on laboriously. I asked them whether they were pleased with their audience, whether His Holiness had addressed them, and the like. The replies came almost in monosyllables. Yes, they were very pleased. Yes, the Holy Father had said a few words, he had received them very cordially and so on. Then there supervened another lull and I began to feel uncomfortable. I wondered what had happened upstairs; had there been some unpleasant hitch or unfortunate blunder, or what else was it that caused this marked restraint and grave demeanour? Thereupon quite abruptly the Prussian Envoy broke the spell: 'Monsignor,' he exclaimed, 'tell us, what is it about this man which attracts us so much?' 'Yes, tell us,' echoed several others.

Somewhat surprised, I asked them whether anything unusual had occurred during the audience and what reason there was for the question addressed to me. No, nothing exceptional had happened. His Holiness, they said, had not detained them very long and at the close of his brief reply to the address presented by their Senior the Holy Father had gone round to greet each one and then had withdrawn, but he left them *sous le charme de sa personnalité*. All I could remark was that I had met His Holiness only a few days since for the first time, that I myself felt impressed by his character and by the charm of his personality. I did not volunteer any explanation. But when the visitors took leave their words remained in my mind and to the question: 'Why does he attract us so much?' I seemed to hear the answer—sanctity, for he is a man of God.

Far from diminishing, this sense of deep veneration and esteem for Pius X continued and increased, as time went on, amongst the members of the Diplomatic Corps. Nor were these sentiments confined to representatives professing the Catholic faith. They appeared to be equally shared and intensely felt by all alike. Even when grave divergences and conflicts arose between the Holy See and their Governments, the special regard and reverence which they entertained for the Holy Father personally was always manifest. He invariably inspired their confidence on every occasion and they gave constant proof of the trust they placed in his unfeigned sincerity and in the elevation and purity of his aims. They realized to the full that when he acted strenuously on behalf of the Church and even showed severity in the measures which he adopted in her defence, he did so without bitterness and purely from a heartfelt sense of his great responsibility.

This was particularly noticeable at the time of his death, and rarely, I fancy, has the death of a Pontiff caused such genuine grief, or such an impression of personal loss among the members of the Diplomatic Corps, as was the case on that occasion. I saw several moved to tears; and I well remember how one of the Envoys, not a Catholic, speaking of the Holy Father the morning after his death and expressing his great sorrow, went on to say that he intended to ask his Government for another post elsewhere, for whoever the new Pontiff might be, Rome would no longer be the same to him without Pius X.

Another of the plenipotentiaries that day, referring to the troubled state of Europe and to the outbreak of the Great War, exclaimed in my presence: 'The last light and hope of peace is extinguished now that Pius X is gone and all is dark on every side.' 'We have had our disagreements and trying moments under the rule of the deceased Pontiff,' said one of the non-Catholic representatives, 'but one always realized the lofty purpose of His Holiness, his appreciation of the difficulties of others and the rectitude of his intentions.'

## IV

## IMPRESSIONS OF STATESMEN CONCERNING PIUS X

PRINCE VON BULOW, as is well known, after retiring from the chancellorship of the German Empire, was in the habit of spending every winter and spring in Rome, where he owned the Villa Malta, and he never failed to ask for an audience with the Holy Father each year on his arrival in the Eternal City and on his departure. He was always immensely struck by his interviews with Pius X and after his reception he invariably expressed to me his admiration for His Holiness, who had astonished him by the shrewdness of his remarks and by the accuracy of his judgement upon men and things. I often heard him comment upon his audience in the following words: 'All that His Holiness said to me this morning is so true, so just. I have met many monarchs and rulers, but I have rarely come across in any one of them such remarkable insight into human nature or the knowledge His Holiness possesses of the forces that govern the world and modern society.'

I have heard it confidently asserted that Prince von Bulow was opposed to the Great War and to the policy which led up to it; I am not in a position to know whether this be true or not; what I can assert beyond doubt is that neither he nor others ever gathered from the lips of Pius X a single word to favour or to justify the tendency to provoke an aggression or the outbreak of violence and that the saintly Pontiff would have given his life-blood to prevent the dreadful conflict and to protect humanity from the untold suffering brought about by the war.

Emile Olivier, the distinguished French statesman, who had occasion to converse at length with the Holy Father in the early days of his pontificate, expressed his appreciation almost in identical terms and then went on to say as was reported in the Press: 'He has not the official majesty of Leo XIII, but he has that of an irresistible gentleness and goodness. What struck me most are the superior gifts of his mind. His intelligence is made of clearness, lucidity and precision. He is a wonderful listener, he rightly understands what is said to him, he goes straight to the decisive and delicate point of a question, which he sums up in a few precise words; no dreamings, no vagaries, but the sense of reality and the knowledge at a glance of what is possible and what is not. And what impressed me even more than the charm and intelligence of Pius X is his fearlessness. He possesses true courage, gentle, calm and free from vaunting. He will never shout a *non possumus*, but when he is compelled to utter it, he will do so in a low voice and then maintain it inflexibly. If difficult circumstances arise, you may expect great things from him. He will be on occasion both a hero and a saint?

Count Goluchowski, Count Sturza, Sir Wilfrid Laurier, Mr. John Redmond and other prominent statesmen and politicians of Europe and of America were hardly less explicit in giving utterance to a similar estimation of the gifts and character of the late Pontiff.

Archbishop Bignami of Syracuse in Sicily, lately deceased, called upon me in December, 1917, to relate a very long conversation he had

had a few days previously with one of Italy's best known Ministers, then in power, whom he happened to have met a few days previously during a journey through the island. That distinguished member of the Government, after discoursing eloquently upon the merits and attainments of Pope Pius X, did not hesitate to declare that in his opinion the general sentiment of the Holy Father's goodness had caused many to overlook his other eminent qualities, which he considered place Pius X deservedly amongst the greatest Pontiffs of the Catholic Church. He himself, he added, had never had occasion to meet His Holiness and therefore had not personally experienced the charm of his goodness, but he judged him by his acts which in many instances he personally had been able to appreciate. This statement I took down in writing from the lips of Monsignor Bignami.

## V

## MY NOMINATION AS CARDINAL SECRETARY OF STATE

It is with great reluctance that I touch upon this event which is so personal to myself, and I should certainly have omitted any reference to it had it not been brought long since to public notice and more or less accurately described by others. Moreover, owing to the indiscretion of an old friend, the text of the letter which His Holiness condescended to address to me on that occasion has already appeared in print, and therefore I have thought that I should not hesitate to tell the story myself, especially as it may further illustrate a characteristic manner of acting on the part of Pius X.

Few perhaps will readily believe the fact, but during the two months and more that elapsed between the day of his election and the morning when he handed me my nomination, Pius X never once gave me an inkling of what was passing in his mind in this connection. The wildest rumours were afloat regarding the person whom it would seem probable that the Holy Father would call to the office of Cardinal Secretary of State and the choice he was most likely to make. Occasionally, I believe, my name was suggested in the Press together with several others, though for cogent and obvious reasons it appeared evident that His Holiness could not possibly be thinking of me, and I must candidly confess that I did not find it within me to consider such a strange and unexpected issue.

The busy weeks passed by. The heavy burden of daily work left no time to think of aught else and could only inspire the wish of being relieved from the crushing responsibility of a temporary office that no reasonable person could surely desire to see prolonged. Later on I learnt that the Holy Father during all that lapse of time had frequently sought the advice of several of the most prominent and experienced members of the Sacred College on this matter and had made it the subject of constant prayer.

On the morning of Sunday, October 18, 1903, I despatched business with His Holiness as usual for about an hour, and when I stood up to take leave he handed me a somewhat bulky envelope addressed to me in his own handwriting, saying quite casually, as if referring to something he had all but forgotten: 'Oh, Monsignor, this is for you.' On previous occasions he had done the same at the end of an audience and more than once he had given me closed envelopes of this kind similarly addressed containing documents that required special attention. I therefore felt no surprise, nor did I attach any exceptional importance to the fact. I slipped the packet into my papers and replied: 'Very good, Holy Father, I will see to it and report tomorrow.'

I was passing along the loggia on the way to my rooms when I was stopped by Cardinal Mocenni, who, it appears, had spoken to His Holiness earlier in the morning and knew what was coming. His Eminence had always been very friendly and kind to me during the eight years I spent in the Vatican under Leo XIII and he was accustomed to treat me familiarly. 'Well, what news have we this morning?' he said, in his rough and ready way. 'Who is going to be the new Cardinal Secretary?' 'I am sure

I don't know, Your Eminence,' was my reply, 'the Holy Father has never made any mention of the matter in my presence.' The Cardinal's face fell and he drew himself up with a gesture of surprise. 'How is that?' he exclaimed rather abruptly. 'Come into my room.' I followed him into his study where he made me sit down and then proceeded to ply me with questions. He declared it impossible that I should be unacquainted with the decision His Holiness had come to. I repeated my assurance that nothing exceptional had marked my interview with the Pope, that not a word had been said of the future Cardinal Secretary, and that I had come away as usual with my papers and an envelope of documents which the Holy Father had given me a moment before. 'An envelope!' he exclaimed. 'Where is it? Why don't you open it?' I proceeded to do so and I glanced through the letter I found there. Is it too much to say that I felt dazed and staggered by its contents?

The old Cardinal looked on with a knowing smile and affectionately patted me on the back. Together with the Pope's autograph there was enclosed a considerable sum in bank-notes, which explained the thickness of the envelope. In his fatherly kindness His Holiness wished me to accept this bounty no doubt because I had hitherto received no salary of any sort and also because he wanted to contribute to the expenses I should incur by my promotion.

The letter ran as follows:

'The opinion of the eminent cardinals who chose you as Secretary of the Conclave, the kindness wherewith you consented to undertake, during this time, the duties of the Secretariate of State, and the devoted care wherewith you have filled this most delicate office, oblige me to ask you to assume permanently the post of my Secretary of State.

'For this reason, and also to satisfy a heartfelt need of my own, and to give you a little token of my warm gratitude, in the forthcoming Consistory of November 9 I shall give myself the pleasure of creating you a cardinal of the Holy Roman Church.

'For your comfort, I may further add that by so doing I shall accomplish an act very acceptable to the majority of the cardinals, who share my admiration of the eminent gifts with which God has enriched you, and with which you will certainly render signal service to the Church.

'To this end, with particular affection, I impart to you the Apostolic Benediction.

'Given at the Vatican the 18th October, 1903.

'Pius P.P. X.'

After recovering to some extent from my dismay, I went up to see the Holy Father, who welcomed me with great affection but firmly set aside any attempt to gainsay his resolution, or to obtain release. He had made up his mind, he assured me, with due deliberation and I must bow to the will of God as he himself had done before me.

## VI

## PIUS X AND THE GREAT WAR

I AM in a position today to testify that His Holiness Pope Pius X repeatedly foretold the outbreak of the Great War in Europe long before the storm actually burst and at a time when few, if any, as far as I am aware, ventured beyond expressing in general terms the fear that sooner or later the growing hostility between preponderant and mighty nations would inevitably result in violent warfare with all its dreadful consequences.

As far back as the years 1911 and 1912, the Holy Father would frequently speak to me of the approaching conflict and he did so more than once in a manner which was almost alarming. On several occasions during the course of those years, four or five times to my recollection, as I entered his room for my morning audience at nine o'clock, His Holiness would open conversation with the following remark:

'Eminence, things are going badly' (*Eminenza, le cose vanno male*). Usually at that hour he had looked through the newspapers and telegrams of the previous evening or early morning, and before dealing with the business of the day, he often made a survey of the general situation and expressed his views regarding the trend of public events. He would draw out historical parallels and dwell upon the unlearnt lessons of the past, upon the similarity of the factors constantly at work at all periods of the world's history with those discernible in our own times, in spite of the ever changing circumstances, whilst above all the restless cravings of the human passions the ruling hand of Providence was perpetually manifest. When the Holy Father discoursed on these subjects, he was at his best.

But he very rarely volunteered any definite forecast. Hence when he so emphatically asserted that 'things were going badly,' I naturally sought to discover the reason of the particularly unfavourable impression he had gathered from the Press or from other sources.

Without attempting to question the fact that there had often been cause for anxiety, I asked the Holy Father on those occasions what it was that had so especially drawn his attention and given rise to the fears he thus expressed. 'Things are going badly,' he invariably replied, 'the Great War is approaching' (*Le cose vanno male, viene il guerrone*). 'I do not mean this war,' he added, at the time of the Italian expedition in Libya and during the Balkan conflict, 'not this, but the Great War . . . *il guerrone.*' Who indeed could deny the possibility of a general conflagration in Europe? Yet, I ventured to point out that it hardly appeared to be in sight in the immediate future: it might still be put off for a long time and perhaps avoided in our day; that in spite of several narrow escapes, those who held the reins of government and who were in a position to control in some measure the course of events, showed undoubtedly how much they hesitated to launch the world along a path of which it was impossible for any man to foresee the final issue.

The Holy Father after listening attentively to my somewhat optimistic remarks, would then raise his hand as if in warning and make the following reply with unusual gravity: 'Eminence, things are going badly, we shall not get beyond the year 1914' (*Eminenza, . . . non passeremo il '14*).

As I have stated, this occurred several times during those years and I remember how on returning to my room I pondered over the words of His Holiness. I sat wondering what grounds he had for thus fixing definitely upon 1914 as the year of the coming war; nor could I find an answer.

I never breathed a word of this to anybody then, for I felt that I was bound to keep the matter to myself. I see no reason now for not acquainting others with this remarkable announcement made to me by the saintly Pontiff and I leave it to them to define its character.

That this forecast was not merely a passing thought is obvious, not only because it was repeatedly uttered in my presence, but also because it is corroborated by another testimony which has come quite recently to my knowledge.

Dr. Bruno Chaves, the Brazilian Minister to the Holy See for many years, resigned his office in 1913. Pope Pius X had always shown him affection and spoke freely to him. In a letter addressed to me from his residence in Pelotas on October 24, 1917, Dr. Chaves refers to his last audience with the Holy Father on May 30, 1913, during which His Holiness said to him: 'You are fortunate, sir, to be going back to your home in Brazil; you will not witness the world-wide war.'

'I thought,' writes Dr. Chaves, 'that His Holiness was alluding to the Balkans, but he went on to say: "The Balkans are the commencement of a great conflagration which I am powerless to avoid and which I shall be unable to resist." I transmitted this apprehension of His Holiness confidentially to some of my friends over here, in the month of August of the same year 1913. Twelve months later it became a sad and cruel reality.' Dr. Chaves' letter is written in Portuguese and the above is a literal translation.

It may well have been in connection with the same foresight that the Holy Father about that time, one day in the Vatican Gardens, as he stood before the shrine of our Lady of Lourdes, exclaimed in the presence of his private chaplain, Monsignor Bressan: 'I pity my successor. I shall not see it, but it is only too true that the *Religio depopulata* is at hand.'

# VII

# CHARACTERISTICS OF PIUS X

The lovable character of Pius X and the kindness of his heart are attested by all who ever came in contact with him, and there is but one voice to extol what is generally spoken of as his 'goodness.' Nor is this indeed to be wondered at. So striking a feature of his individuality could not fail to impress the minds of the thousands who approached him during the eleven years of his pontificate, not to mention all those who had experienced the unfailing charity and sweet devotedness of the humble village curate in Tombolo, of the parish priest in Salzano, or who had known him intimately when he laboured in their midst as Chancellor of Treviso, Bishop of Mantua and Cardinal Patriarch of Venice.

Add to this his fatherly interest in every case of trouble or of suffering that happened to come before him, the generous help of his advice and counsel even in matters that might well seem trifling except to those concerned, the material assistance and liberal subsidies that he lavished both in public and in private, with such extreme delicacy of regard for the feelings of those he benefited, and it will be readily understood why the 'goodness' of Pius X will never be forgotten and why so many are content to speak only of this conspicuous lineament of his personality, which so truly reflected the love of the Divine Master.

But to imagine that this attractive characteristic in Pius X describes the man or in any way sums up his gifts and powers would be an utter misapprehension; nothing could be further from the truth. Coupled with that 'goodness' and happily blended with the tenderness of a father's heart, there was in him an indomitable strength of character and an energy of will to which all must testify who really knew him, but which not infrequently surprised or even startled those who had only experienced the constant proofs of his habitual gentleness and restraint.

He held himself in complete control and quelled the impulses of his ardent temperament. He was quick to give way in matters which were not essential and ever ready to consider and accept the opinion of others where no principle was at stake; but weakness in him there was none.

When one or other grave question arose in which the rights and liberty of the Church required to be stated and upheld, when the purity and integrity of Catholic truth stood in need of assertion and defence, or ecclesiastical discipline had to be maintained in the face of laxity or worldly influence, then Pius X would reveal the full strength and energy of his character and the fearless vigour of a great ruler conscious of the responsibility of his sacred office and of the duties he felt called upon to fulfil at any cost. It was idle then for anybody to endeavour to shake his constancy; every effort to intimidate him by threats or to cajole him by specious pleas and appeals to mere sentiment was inevitably doomed to failure. On such occasions, after days of anxious thought and many a sleepless night, I have seen him slowly close his hand as it rested on his desk, until it was firmly clenched, and then raising his head, with a severe and dauntless look in his eyes that were habitually so calm and gentle, he would express his definite resolution or deliver judgement in few and measured terms. One knew then that there was nothing more to say.

Lest it should be thought that perhaps I have overestimated this side of the Holy Father's character and that my appreciation may be biassed by my affection, it will not be out of place to recall here the testimony of others, who, though undoubtedly much less in contact with Pius X than I have been, were however in a position to form an opinion deserving of attention, based upon their personal knowledge and experience. Monsignor Baudrillart, of the French Academy and Rector of the Catholic Institute in Paris, writes as follows in an article in the *Revue Pratique d'Apologétique* which is well worth reading in its entirety:

'His look, his word, his whole being express three things: goodness, firmness, faith. Goodness was the man himself; firmness was the leader; faith was the Christian, the priest, the pontiff, the man of God. "*Tu autem, O homo Dei.*" This exclamation of the apostle rushed to one's lips from the heart, when one was admitted to this Pope's presence. How far away one was from human manœuvres and political devices! How sure one was that one would hear nothing but the word of God from his mouth! How impossible one knew it would be to resort to the slightest equivocation or diplomatic ingenuity in his presence! One told him things just as they were, quite simply, and waited for his reply, with the firm resolve to do whatever he should say, to the best of one's power.

'There were times when that answer seemed somewhat hard! With what energy would the Pope order us to root out the weeds from that part of the Church which he had entrusted to our care! We looked at him; we read in his sad gentle eyes, light in their depths but veiled with a shadow, words such as these: "I, too, suffer, I suffer more than you do, for I have to act in every direction to repress and to strike, I the father, the father of all; but that is the duty of my office, the duty I cannot escape; the Church's peril urges me on, peril from without, and yet worse peril from within; have I any right to consider whether I suffer?" . . . Pius X was the most supernatural of men; that *Deus providebit* (God will provide) which was for ever on his lips is the very expression of his whole religious and moral being. And that is why, once he was certain that his duty was to act in this or that way, he paid no further heed to the consequences, confident that God would draw a greater and lasting good from a lesser and passing evil.

'He had the clear vision of the upright; and a clear vision that no falsehood or sophistry or hypocrisy could manage to deceive. . . . Quietly with unshaken calm he denounced and condemned evil wherever he saw it; no consideration could make him bend. . . . Pius X showed himself a ruler. His name will remain for ever linked with the reorganizing of the Roman Courts and Congregations, and the codifying of Canon Law, a colossal work soon completed, which will bring simplicity, light, strength, and unity into the government of the Church.

'No Pope was ever more a reformer, no more modern, than this fearless adversary of Modernist errors. Faithful to his watchword, he undertook to restore and renew everything in Jesus Christ.

'Governments may have feared or set themselves against him. He was loved, tenderly loved by the people, by all the good and simple faithful, because he was a saint, because he was a father.'[1]

Not less striking or emphatic in this respect are the words of His Eminence Cardinal Mercier in his Lenten Pastoral of February 2, 1915. I may be allowed to quote the following extract:

'The winning kindness of the Holy Father had none of the soft sentimentality of the weak. Pius X was strong. It is currently reported that he was the writer of a short prayer which priests have to say at certain times for their bishop. It runs as follows: "*Oremus pro Antistite nostro N* (Let us also pray for our Bishop). *Stet et pascat in fortitudine tua, Domine, in sublimitate nominis tui.* (Strong in Thy strength, O Lord,

---

[1] *Revue Pratique d'Apologétique*, 15 Août-1 Septembre, 1914.

let him stand and feed the flock in the sublimity of Thy name)."

'And this, unless I am mistaken, is the characteristic note of the late Pope—a wonderful combination of fatherly tenderness with a force of character that made him master of himself and imparted to his soul steadiness of equilibrium, filling his expression with that blending of gravity, serenity, condescension, and almost of playfulness, which so strongly attracted everyone by its charm.

'The public looked on with wonder, sometimes with anxiety, and admired the virile Pontiff in his hand-to-hand struggle with Modernism.

'In the days of Luther and Calvin, had the Church possessed a Pope of the temper of Pius X, would Protestantism have succeeded in getting one-third of Europe to break loose from Rome?

'Pius was a man of keen insight and decision. He would not let himself be seduced by the cajoleries of reformers, naïvely ambitious of infusing the veins of the Church with new blood, and dreaming of modernizing her to suit the fancies and errors of up-to-date Protestantism and Rationalism. True to Catholic Tradition, he blazoned forth the axiom that in the fifth century, St. Vincent of Lerins, himself the disciple of a martyr-bishop of the third century, St. Cyprian, used against those who favoured a doctrinal advance which the Christian conscience would have felt to be not an improvement but a revolution, wherein all the treasures of the past would have disappeared: *Nihil innovetur nisi quod traditum est* (No innovations: cleave to tradition).

'His plan once laid down, the Pope pursued it, both as a whole and in detail, in the sphere of doctrine and also of discipline, in scientific works, in the Press, in literature, in the teaching of Seminaries and of Universities and even in the persons of those whom he loved most; he pursued its fullest realization, I say, with an energy and perseverance that were sometimes disconcerting.

'When we survey from afar this line of action, many-sided yet one, broad and yet penetrating, we are unanimous in our admiration of our great Pope's force of character, and in thanking Providence for saving Christianity from an immense peril, not only of a single heresy but of all heresies combined, amalgamated together in a more or less treacherous way.'[1]

We have evidence of this spirit and strength in weighty Encyclicals and in various enactments issued by Pius X during the whole course of his pontificate, in his public allocutions, in his frequent addresses and exhortations of all kinds, and also in his private correspondence.

It is well to state here that the Holy Father very often wrote out the minutes of important documents or furnished copious notes and material for their compilation. Several of these neatly penned autographs, as well as many private or unpublished letters of his, are in my possession and I am able to quote from his own manuscripts.

Remarkable among others is the short and characteristic exhortation which he addressed to the French Bishops whom he himself had consecrated in St. Peter's, at the altar of the

---

[1] *Lettre Pastorale et mandement de Carême de* 1915.

'Cathedra,' on February 25, 1906, after the rupture of the Concordat by the French Government. Unrecognized and unassisted, they were going forth to fight their battle and nobody could foresee what awaited them. Pius X received them privately in his library, where he wished me to be present, and spoke as follows:

'I was anxious to see you all assembled in order to address a word of confidence and affection to you, under the seal of secrecy, and to tell you how much I value the great sacrifice that you have undertaken of facing poverty, privations, and even, which God forbid, of not only seeing your authority discarded, of being persecuted.

'This very day you will receive instructions regarding the line of action you are to adopt on your impending return and on taking possession of the dioceses confided to your care. I do not urge the exact observance of what will be suggested to you, for I should be doing injury to your sentiments of obedience and reverence towards every direction of the Holy Apostolic See.

## CHARACTERISTICS OF PIUS X

'In due time you will be called upon to attend the general assembly of all the French Bishops, to express your judgement upon the law, as soon as the Regulations are published, *viz.*: whether and under what conditions it is suitable to endure the law, whether and how the law should be resisted, etc.

'It is not improbable that during your present stay in Rome you may have heard mentioned or even received suggestions upon the subject. I recommend that you should take no notice of this, because the Pope, who hitherto has refrained from revealing his judgement to anybody, before uttering the last word, wishes to hear the views of all the Bishops, free entirely as they are to express their mind upon what they deem best for the glory of God, for the salvation of souls, for the honour of the clergy and for the security of religion in France.

'All that I recommend to you is that in the coming conference of Bishops, when giving your vote in reply to the questions submitted to you, (1) you should conform yourselves to the spirit of Jesus Christ, *quacumque humana postposita*. (2) You should reflect that we are born to strife: *non veni pacem mittere, sed gladium*. (3) In forming your judgement you should consider the spirit of true Catholics in your country. (4) You should safeguard the essential principles of justice and defend the rights of the Church, which are the rights of God. (5) You should bear in mind not only the judgement of God, but also that of the world that has its eyes upon you, if ever you were to belie your dignity or fail in the duties it lays upon you.

'And here I conclude with the assurance that I envy your lot, that I would fain come with you to share your sorrows and anxieties, to be ever at your side to comfort you. But though absent in body, I shall be constantly near you in spirit, and we shall meet each day in the divine sacrifice of the Mass, before the holy Tabernacle whence we derive strength in battle and the sure means of victory.'

There was nobody else present besides myself at this meeting which the Holy Father held in his private library, two days after the grand ceremony of the Consecration in St. Peter's. In contrast with his usual practice, he had committed this short address to memory, but he read it from his own manuscript in a solemn tone, and dwelt upon each word to emphasize the importance of what he wished to convey to his hearers.

Though the same energy and strength of character were not absent by any means from his dealings with individual cases in which he could not avoid administering reproof or punishment without failing in the accomplishment of a solemn duty, the severity of Pius X on such occasions was ever coupled with the tenderness of his fatherly affection, and, when obliged to cause distress to those at fault, he felt for the guilty and their pain was his.

As an instance, among several others, I can well remember how one morning the Holy Father confided to me that he was about to receive in audience a person who had very grievously erred and had betrayed his sacred duty. It was a sad story. The Pope's direct intervention had become inevitable, for the delinquent had thrown off all restraint and seemed little inclined to repent or accept correction. I found His Holiness looking very sad and tired. He acknowledged to me that he had spent a restless night thinking over the approaching interview and the necessity of his speaking with the utmost severity. He was however determined to carry the matter through, he said, but it would cost him a great deal, for he realized what a blow it would undoubtedly be for the unfortunate culprit. 'Say a Hail Mary for me, Eminence,' he added, 'in order that God may bless this audience and that the poor fellow may not rebel and force me to go further.'

A few hours later the Holy Father was beaming with joy. 'Do you know, all went well,' he exclaimed, with a smile. 'The unhappy man ended by acknowledging the truth of all I said. I did not spare him, but, thank God, he has submitted and now we must do what we can to help him on.'

When he thus inflicted correction, the severity of his countenance and the solemn resonance of his voice were most impressive and generally produced an overwhelming impression upon the person who had incurred his displeasure, but his was the anger of the lamb, the anger that sinneth not.

Sickness, fatigue or pain endured by others, especially by persons whom he knew more intimately or whose services he employed, even in menial offices, infallibly aroused his deepest sympathy, nor did he seem to rest until assured that they had found relief. 'Do not worry over the . . .' he would write, 'you have made good provision for that, and worry still less over me, for, enjoying sufficient health, as I do, I always live contented and happy in the well-being of those who are dear to me; whereas the fear alone that they should suffer causes me anguish. Therefore be of good heart.' Or again: 'You must not be anxious on account of the fears expressed by the Rev. N. N. The choice was made after full consideration and let us trust that the Lord will bless his apostolate. In any event, however, the responsibility is not solely yours, but mine also and we shall share it in peace. Therefore be of good heart.'

And yet, though nothing could surpass the sensibility of his affectionate temperament, in Pius X there was no trace of weak sentimentality or of unreasonable emotion. As Cardinal Mercier rightly says, Pius X had a strong character. If others lost control over their feelings and gave way in his presence to an excessive display of mere sentiment, '*Esto vir* . . . be a man,' was the reply which rose constantly to his lips and which he accompanied with a firm and energetic gesture. Indeed it is my opinion that the sheer sense of humour, which he certainly possessed, would alone have sufficed to prevent him from allowing his emotions to gain the mastery beyond the limits of reason.

I may illustrate this remark by an anecdote. In 1912, the restored Campanile of Saint Mark's, Venice, was to be solemnly inaugurated. The Holy Father had naturally taken the keenest interest in the reconstruction of this historic monument, so dear to the heart of every Venetian. He had himself laid the first stone of the new building and, no doubt, many cherished memories lingered in his mind in connection with the old Campanile. He had carefully followed the progress of the work through all its stages and he had made a gift of one of the new bells.

Shortly before the joyful celebration that was to commemorate the completion of the great enterprise, a report went about in the Press that the Italian Government intended setting up a direct telephone wire between Venice and the Vatican, in order to enable His Holiness to hear the chime of Saint Mark's. Then followed the announcement that the Pope's medical advisers had intervened and put an end to the proposal on the grounds, it was asserted, that the Holy Father would experience too intense emotion and that this might prove detrimental to his health. He was very much amused by all this gossip.

As a matter of fact the idea of asking the Italian Government to provide a direct telephone line from Venice to the Vatican had been suggested by some eager friends of the former Patriarch, but Pius X set the proposal aside, so he told me himself, nor had the doctors held it their duty to interfere, nor had any fear been expressed regarding the impression likely to be produced upon His Holiness' feelings.

He laughed heartily over the whole story and commenting upon it, with a merry twinkle in his eye, he said: 'Do they take me for a young lady? I did not consent to the suggestion made by those good folk, among other reasons, to tell the truth, because in all probability I should have been the last person to hear anything distinctly. You may be sure that the line would have been tapped and I should have heard little or nothing. Moreover, I have to listen to bells enough in Rome, and indeed too many.'

When making this remark, the Holy Father was alluding perhaps to the endless tolling of the bells of St. Peter's, in close proximity to his own rooms and which on certain occasions proved somewhat trying. But those familiar with the Italian expression *sentire troppe campane* will realize that he was referring chiefly to the inevitable conflict of opinions, appeals and complaints with which he had constantly to deal.

He had a cheerful, loving heart, a strong and manly will, and it was this disposition, supported by his confidence in God, which helped him to bear so bravely the weight and worry of his arduous office.

# VIII

## HIS LEARNING AND ELOQUENCE

We need hardly wish for more reliable information regarding the early years and education of the late Pontiff than that which Canon Marchesan of Treviso has carefully collected and published in his *Life of Pius X*.

There the author bears testimony to Giuseppe Sarto's proficiency in the study of the classics and to his literary attainments, which won for him the praise of his teachers, and of which he subsequently gave abundant proof in numberless discourses, addresses, sermons and pastoral letters, as well as in his private correspondence.

Pius X was far too deeply engrossed in the pastoral work for which he lived, as a parish priest, as Bishop and as Supreme Pontiff, to be able to dedicate any considerable portion of his time to literary or artistic pursuits; nevertheless, when occasion arose, he revealed the gifts and tastes of a cultured mind both in literature and in art. He had read extensively. Holy Scripture, theology and history seemed to be the subjects he preferred, and even amidst the daily cares and incessant labour of his exalted office, he managed, I could see, to peruse many a volume and to keep in touch with modern thought. Time and again he surprised me by his accurate knowledge of distant nations and peoples, of their traditions, customs and special character; hence the facility with which he could gauge a situation and appreciate the views and feelings predominant in countries so different from his own and which he had never visited. To say nothing of nations regarding which information is more generally within reach, his grasp, for instance, of the intricate questions connected with the Slavs, their liturgy and national aspirations was often remarkable, and this no doubt was due in great measure to the knowledge he had acquired by coming in contact with many representatives of those nationalities during the nine years he spent in Venice.

Recent publications in Italian or French on various subjects were constantly before him. French he could read without any difficulty and with real pleasure, though he was always shy of speaking in that language, chiefly, I imagine, because he could not master the pronunciation and accent. Nevertheless on some occasions I have known him to carry on a private conversation in French, and once, just after the solemn Beatification of Joan of Arc, when hundreds of French pilgrims assembled in St. Peter's for their great reception, he agreeably surprised them by delivering a lengthy reply to their address of homage, in their own tongue. He had written the original text in Italian and ordered a translation.

In the hope of inducing His Holiness to overcome his reluctance to speaking in French and to be more confident in his ability to do so I remember telling him what had occurred to me a few days previously. One of the Envoys accredited to the Holy See, who was certainly not a French scholar, wishing to impress upon me that feeling was running high in his country in regard to a hotly debated question, assured me that *les animaux sont très agités là bas*. He had evidently got hold of the Italian expression *gli animi sono molto agitati* and had translated *animi* into *animaux* instead of *esprits*. Of course it was as much as I could do to preserve my gravity. I argued that after all if a Minister could afford to make such blunders in an official interview, surely the Holy Father need not feel shy of an occasional slip in private conversation. But far from convincing His Holiness or encouraging him not to be deterred by the casual mistakes he might commit in the use of a foreign tongue, my argument led him to draw the opposite conclusion. Laughing heartily at the anecdote, he exclaimed: 'Now you see why I do not run such risks. It would be rather dreadful, you know, for a Pope to talk such nonsense.' I could not say that he was wrong.

Monsignor Sarto's funeral oration on the death of Monsignor Rota, Bishop of Mantua, is an excellent specimen of his style and of the care and precision with which he wrote. I think that if some at least of his numerous other compositions were published and more widely known, Pius X's command of language and literary taste would be further appreciated.

He handled his pen with remarkable ease and rapidity. His handwriting was particularly neat and he would draw up whole pages of a minute with very few corrections. In the midst of other work, frequently between one audience and another, he would send me a note, either to transmit or to ask for urgent information, to make a suggestion or to give his orders. Very many of these autographs are still in my possession. They are all neatly written, without an erasure, accurately punctuated, dated and addressed. It was indeed a mystery to me how he managed to pen and despatch them with such rapidity in the course of a morning, when he had not a moment to himself and whilst audiences and work of all kinds crowded in upon him without interruption. I ventured more than once to remonstrate with him and to beg that he would ring or send for me in order to save himself unnecessary fatigue: 'No,' he replied, 'we are both of us too busy to waste time and it is quicker for me to write.'

The admirable *Exhortatio ad Clerum*, which the Holy Father dedicated to the clergy throughout the world in memory of his sacerdotal jubilee, he wrote out page by page during intervals of spare time in little over a fortnight.

As day by day the work progressed, he condescended to read it to me and to invite criticism. It was exclusively his own personal effort and it was truly a labour of love. In the short preface to the English edition Cardinal Bourne most aptly declares: 'The words of the saintly Pius X, written to his fellow Priests on the fiftieth anniversary of his own ordination to the priesthood, should be held in constant remembrance by all who have been called to the service of the Altar. They are the outpourings of the heart of a true Priest fashioned to the likeness of his Master as Priest and Bishop, and under the burden of the Supreme Pontificate. May the burning words of the holy Pontiff, for eleven years Christ's Vicar upon the earth, restore, strengthen and make permanent in the hearts of all His Priests the fundamental teachings which these words set forth.'

What may be styled the more formal and official pronouncements of His Holiness, such as Allocutions to the Sacred College, Apostolic Letters and the like, were not habitually drawn up by him, though in fact for the compilation of these weighty documents he would frequently write out drafts or furnish notes, and he never failed to give precise instruction or to carefully revise every portion of the work prepared for him by his subordinates.

But, for instance, the stirring address of Pius X to the newly elected Cardinals in the Consistory of May, 1914, subsequently published in the *Acta Apostolicæ Sedis*, was his own composition from start to finish and written in his own hand. I possess the manuscript of this his last oration, delivered immediately after bestowing the red 'biretta' upon the recently appointed members of the Sacred College, among whom stood the Archbishop of Bologna, Cardinal Della Chiesa. The memory of this telling allocution, within three months of his death, so manifestly inspired by his apostolic zeal and worthy of a great Pontiff, must be fresh in the minds of many, for it produced the deepest impression upon all present.

The same may be said of a number of other speeches directed to public bodies of different kinds. On such occasions the Holy Father would either read the written document he had prepared, or speak with his manuscript in his hand, though he hardly did more than glance at it in the course of delivery.

Not a few are inclined to think that as a speaker Pius X was often at his best when extemporizing, which he frequently did. His words came fluently in correct sentences and in language full of significance, bereft of all artificial rhetoric or empty phraseology. That he felt intensely everything he said, none of his hearers could ever doubt; and it was this earnestness, together with the rich harmony of his voice, with the dignity of his gestures and the light of his countenance that riveted attention, lent exquisite charm to his diction and renewed the convincing force of familiar argument.

Monsignor Touchet, the distinguished Bishop of Orleans, himself a brilliant speaker, did not disguise his sincerest admiration for the Holy Father's oratory which he had many opportunities of appreciating during his visit to Rome. He loved to hear him speak. Moreover, he made a point of sending his chief discourses and writings to Pius X and delighted in the shrewd criticism of them which the Holy Father used to make and often communicated to

## HIS LEARNING AND ELOQUENCE

him in a friendly correspondence. An extract from the reply of His Holiness to an address read by Monsignor Touchet in the *Sala del Concistoro* at the time of the Beatification of Joan of Arc will not be out of place here.

I take it from the rough copy, just as it flowed from the Holy Father's pen, and I endeavour in my translation to leave untouched as far as possible the characteristic features of the original text. It was on the morning of April 20, 1909, before a large assembly that the Pope after some preliminary passages went on to say:

'O venerable brethren and beloved sons, who in the accomplishment of the duties of your profession, preach and practise without human respect the teachings of the Catholic Church, and, for this very reason, not only endure contempt and scorn, but are held up to public censure and branded as enemies of your country, cast back in the face of cowardly slanderers this libel that so deeply wounds the hearts of Catholics and which it requires the full power of divine grace for you to forgive in those who so basely offend you.

'If Catholicism were an enemy of our fatherland it would not be a divine religion. Fatherland is a sacred name that recalls to mind our dearest memories and, whether it be because we are of one blood with those born in the same place, or because of the nobler similarity of affections and traditions, our country is worthy not only of love but of predilection. And if this be the case everywhere, much more must it be so when our country is linked by ties indissoluble to that fatherland which is not restricted within the boundaries of any ocean or encompassed by mountain ranges, which speaks not one but all tongues, the fatherland which comprises in its latitude the visible world and the world beyond the grave—the Catholic Church! To politicians who detect an enemy in the Church and therefore perpetually oppose her, to sectarians who with all the hatred inspired by Satan unceasingly calumniate, vilify and attack her, to the false champions of science who by sophistry of every kind strive to render her objectionable, as if she were a foe to liberty, to civilization and to intellectual progress, reply that the Church, mistress of souls and ruling the hearts of men, exercises her supremacy throughout the world because she alone, being the bride of Christ and having all in common with her divine spouse, is the depositary of the truth, she alone can win from all nations veneration and love. Thus he who rebels against her authority for fear lest it should encroach upon the dominion of the State, sets up barriers to the truth; he who proclaims her authority to be foreign to a nation, wishes truth to be foreign to that nation also; he who dreads that her authority may diminish the freedom and greatness of a people, manifestly believes that a nation can be great and free without the truth. Hence if a State, a Government, an Authority, whatever be its name, wage war against the truth, it cannot hope to inspire love whilst opposing the most sacred of human sentiments. That Authority may maintain itself by sheer force, it may be feared because the sword of punishment compels obeisance, it may be applauded out of hypocrisy, interest or servility, it will even be obeyed, because Religion ennobles our subjection to earthly powers, provided they do not exact any thing contrary to the divine law; in which case everyone must withdraw without thereby becoming a rebel. Nevertheless, though this duty of submission in that which is not opposed to the duties prescribed by Religion will render obedience more meritorious, it cannot suffice to make obedience affectionate, joyful and spontaneous, such as to deserve the name of love and veneration.

'We feel veneration therefore for the fatherland which in sweet union with the Church provides for the true welfare of humanity. And that is the reason why champions and saviours of a country have always sprung from the ranks of the best Catholics and that the Saints are invoked in the hymns of our Sacred Liturgy as Fathers of their country; they followed the example of the Saint above all Saints, who, whilst He obeyed those in authority and paid the tribute to Cæsar, on approaching Jerusalem and foreseeing her coming ruin, shed tears in abundance over her, because, beloved and favoured by God, she had not availed herself of so many graces and of the visitation He Himself had made in order to bestow every kind of blessing upon her.'

# IX

## PIUS X AND THE ARTS

THE Church has always granted generous patronage to art wherever her influence has extended. Rome bears eloquent testimony in that respect to the traditional munificence of her Pontiffs and to their enlightened efforts, not only to preserve the monuments of antiquity and the countless relics of past ages, whether pagan or Christian, but also to encourage the activity of artists who afforded proof of genuine talent. And this has been noteworthy even during troubled periods of history whilst Pontiffs were harassed by financial straits and overburdened by the cares of their apostolic ministry.

Nevertheless it is obvious that, taken individually, not every Pope has been gifted personally with an artistic temperament, nor always inclined by education to entertain any special interest in art.

I have already remarked that Pius X was too entirely absorbed, as a priest and pastor, by his zeal and activity for the welfare of souls, to spend any considerable portion of his time in other pursuits, however much they might arouse his interest. But he loved beautiful things, and he had seen many in the course of his life at Mantua, Padua and Venice, and also during his occasional visits to Rome. He enjoyed the friendship of several distinguished artists, whom he always gladly welcomed with a view of improving his knowledge, and his relations with them, together with what he had read, contributed no doubt to educate his taste, which was excellent and refined, at times almost severe.

The Exhibition of Sacred Art held in Venice, in the beautiful church of SS. John and Paul, owed its origin to the initiative and encouragement of the Patriarch, Cardinal Sarto, who took infinite pains to ensure its success.

In this connection I may place on record his habit of recalling how wonderfully the teachings of the Catholic Faith are illustrated in the priceless treasures of ancient Christian art, so lavishly scattered throughout Italy, and how the Masters of old were imbued with the true spirit of the Church. 'In modern Italy,' he frequently said, 'the life and feeling of that sublime language is dormant and requires to be awakened once again.'

He strongly deprecated any negligence in the proper custody of artistic and historical treasures. The circulars he repeatedly issued or suggested to the clergy in Italy and abroad, giving precise instructions and practical rules in this direction, deserve more attention than I fear they have always met with.

That museums and art galleries are indispensable for the preservation of priceless heirlooms, which if lost or deteriorated can never be replaced, he readily granted. But he looked upon them as an objectionable necessity, which he fain would see supplied if possible in a different way. For he held that artistic and historical works should be left in the framework to which they properly belong and that to detach them from it often mars the effect which their authors had in view. Moreover, in his judgement, the distribution throughout the country of the inspired products of human genius and the records of the past, served to cultivate, more than anything else, the taste of the people

## PIUS X AND THE ARTS

and to call forth the natural gifts of born artists in our own day. When the lesson, he said, has to be sought within privileged walls of a museum, chiefly in large towns, on rare occasions, entailing trouble and expense, few can really benefit by it, and the gradual process of unconscious assimilation that prevailed in the past can no longer exist in our own time.

On March 28, 1909, Pius X opened the new gallery which he had taken so much pains to erect for the better and safer custody of the celebrated pictures of the Vatican collection. Many must still remember the old 'Pinacoteca' on the third floor of the Palace. Often, of an afternoon, during the brief intervals of rest or recreation which the Holy Father allowed himself, especially at the beginning of his laborious pontificate, he would wander into the picture gallery, situated then, as will be remembered, on the upper loggia of the Vatican, on a level with His Holiness' private apartments.

Pius X was impressed at once by the fact that the gallery as it then existed, did not afford sufficient space for all the pictures, many of which were crowded together, and that it could not be considered worthy of so important a collection. Moreover, looking due north and exposed to the cold 'tramontana' winds, the low temperature of the rooms proved detrimental to several of the older and more delicate panels, and their proximity to the roof and to living apartments did not provide proper security in case of fire or of other accidents.

The Holy Father spoke to me repeatedly of all this with the deepest concern. He had, however, a further object in view when he determined to erect the new 'Pinacoteca.' The many valuable paintings to be found either in the Vatican Library, in the Lateran Museum or in various halls throughout the Palace, where they almost escaped notice, had attracted his attention. He accordingly suggested the plan of gathering them together, with the purpose of affording wider facilities for the study of the great Masters and of forming a picture gallery more in keeping with the best traditions of the Roman Pontiffs. Such was the idea of Pius X, and the perseverance with which he carried it into effect furnishes evidence of his intelligent interest in the cultivation and progress of art.

## PIUS X AND THE ARTS

Let me mention here that he had very definite ideas regarding the decoration that he considered admissible in churches of real artistic value. Benedict XIV in his classical treatise on the *Beatification and Canonization of the Servants of God* discusses under the heading *Ornatus Vaticani Templi*,[1] the temporary adornments with which it is usual to deck the great Basilica. That illustrious Pontiff justifies the established custom by remarking that the exceptional character of these ornamentations helps to impress the onlooker with the solemnity of the celebration. For our interest is naturally less awakened by what is constantly beneath our gaze, however beautiful it may be, *ab assuetis non fit passio*; and undoubtedly we realize better the full significance of a festival when we see some unwonted decoration adopted for the occasion. Pius X showed no inclination to question this

---

[1] 'Quia tamen minus animum movent quæ praeocul is semper sunt, templa consuevimus, etsi arte et materia apprime nobilia, cum statæ quædam aut extra ordinem celebritates inciderint, adscito cultu et temporariis ornamentis excolere, ut novitas commendet quod assiduitate quomodo viluerat.' (Bened XIV Op: de Servorum Dei Beatificatione et Canonizatione, t. VII.)

view as a general principle, but he very strongly objected to its indiscriminate and exaggerated application.

'For goodness' sake, respect the architectural lines of our churches and the harmony of their design: do not ruin their beauty with your red rags (*stracci rossi*).' This remonstrance I have often heard repeated by Pius X in relation to the excessive use of cheap draperies and flimsy hangings, frequently conspicuous in churches and chapels, even in Rome, on the occasion of great festivals. He frankly censured the extensive covering up of marble walls, stately pillars and fine arches of our sacred edifices, which have little to hide and so much to admire. He held it inconsistent in a way to disguise their splendour with tawdry trappings precisely during those solemn days which afforded the best opportunity for cultivating the taste of the multitudes and for leading them to appreciate the genuine beauty of the house of God.

During the eleven years of the reign of Pius X, a considerable number of new churches were built in and about Rome. Several of them were erected entirely at the expense of His Holiness;

to all he contributed munificently, and the plans of their design were in most cases submitted to his criticism and approval. The urgent requirements of the vast and densely populated quarters in the suburbs of the city, or of the rural districts, made it absolutely necessary to provide places of worship and new parishes for the people. 'There are plenty of fine churches in Rome and yet they do not suffice by any means,' the Holy Father was wont to say. 'I wish I could remove a dozen of them from the centre to the outskirts of the town, for then we should not stand in need of new ones.'

When discussing with the architects, he would go into every detail of the plans they brought him and study them at length and with the greatest care before allowing them to begin the construction. His experience as a parish priest served him in good stead in regard to the practical arrangement and right accommodation of the buildings. With the object of facilitating the work of the ministry ever present in his mind, he made a point of erecting a presbytery attached to the church, and wherever possible he insisted upon having a school in the neighbourhood, a hall for parochial meetings, club work and the like. He did not encourage new ventures in the style of church building, especially in Rome, and he showed a marked preference for the best samples of classical architecture, which he urged should be copied within the limits of reasonable adaptation and expense. 'Why look so far for new designs?' he would exclaim. 'Take some of the old basilicas for a model; there are such splendid churches here around, and there are many more all over the country which it would be difficult to rival; better reproduce the old ones on a larger or smaller scale than waste time in devising ugly novelties of an eccentric or indefinite style.'

But besides painting and architecture other crafts and industries of skill and beauty appealed also to the artistic inclinations of Pius X and gave him opportunities to reveal his powers of observation and the refinement of his tastes. The art of lacemaking was one of these, nor indeed can we wonder that he should have been attracted to it, Venetian as he was, and considering the keen interest he felt in all that shed lustre upon the land of his birth. Canon

Marchesan has published the text of an autograph left by the Patriarch, Cardinal Sarto, at Murano on the occasion of a visit he made to the lace factory there on January 12, 1898. He set himself to encourage the enterprise with the twofold object of favouring its progress and of providing for the moral improvement and spiritual assistance of the many destitute girls he came across in different parts of the city. The Latin circular he issued to his clergy shortly after taking possession of the patriarchal see affords evidence of this, no less than the characteristic autograph which may be rendered in English as follows: 'On visiting the school for lace-making at Murano, I am surprised at the beauty of the work, so kindly shown me, and truly satisfied with the discipline of the establishment, where nearly four hundred girls, in the midst of their difficult and arduous labour, practise the virtues of Christian life. I express the hope that the directors and patrons of the school may find the means of selling this marvellous work and thus provide for the welfare of the artisans and for the needs of this very poor locality.'

An extensive knowledge of the various schools and methods of lace-making at home and abroad enabled him to discourse with proficiency upon the intricacies of *merletti a piombino, punto in aria, panto tagliato* or *punto a reticella*; nor did he experience any difficulty in detecting at a glance the merits or defects of lace which happened to come under his notice, for instance, when altar linen, a rochet or an alb were presented for his acceptance. I cannot help thinking that the donors, would often have felt embarrassed had they realized how accurately he could appreciate and criticize perhaps the exact merit and value of the gifts they offered him.

## X

## PIUS X AND MUSIC

THAT Pius X loved music, for which he possessed a natural talent, is not open to doubt. He had managed to acquire considerable knowledge of the technicalities of the art, and to have achieved this during the course of his busy life warrants the conclusion that he was gifted by nature in that respect, for all the absorbing duties of the ministry allowed him little or no leisure for cultivating his taste. Not many people realize, I imagine, how great the sacrifice often is for a priest to be cut off by his vocation from the enjoyment of hearing really good music. I am sure the Holy Father keenly felt the loss, though he probably did not stop to dwell upon it more than on any other of the advantages he had willingly foregone in the service of the Divine Master. Bad and noisy music, in and out of church, he undoubtedly was obliged to endure all the year round wherever he lived; hence it is surprising that in spite of that he preserved such excellent taste and entertained marked preference for the best style of musical composition, whether sacred or profane.

I recollect how intensely he enjoyed listening to Perosi's great oratorio, 'The Last Judgement,' which by his own wish was executed under the personal direction of the author in the Sala Regia. Flow he commented upon the inspired rendering of the Scriptural texts, the richness of the orchestral parts, without failing to point out the qualities or deficiencies he had noted here or there either in the composition itself or in the singers. He experienced even more pleasure in the glorious chant of several hundred voices during the solemn Pontifical Mass which he sung in St. Peter's for the centenary of the great St. Gregory; many will long remember that memorable day.

It would not be in keeping with the limited scope of these sketches for me to dwell at any length upon the efforts made by Pius X to re-establish sacred music according to the time-honoured traditions and spirit of the Catholic Church; it would be superfluous, too, for his public utterances and instructions on this subject have been widely circulated and a great deal has been written to illustrate their importance. I cannot omit however some mention of his ideas and guidance in that respect inasmuch as they came to my personal notice. Here again the foremost aim of his life inspired his judgement and directed his action. He appreciated good music of every kind, but sacred music naturally interested him most. He would insist upon procuring the best, which, in his eyes, could only be music that was really sacred and eminently 'artistic,' in harmony with the liturgy of the Church and the genuine expression of the sentiments that faith inspires. Its purpose must be that of an auxiliary to devotion. Without questioning in many cases its innate beauty, he held that it was out of place if, instead of leading us to God as a means and a help to prayer, it became excessively prominent and ceased to be subsidiary to the final and paramount object of worship, the raising up of our minds and hearts to God.

He strongly maintained the principle that if music is to render its tribute of praise and homage to God, it must not be of inferior quality and that we should strive to produce the very best. On the other hand he was fully aware that in order to bring about a lasting reform in church music, merely disciplinary measures, however stringent, cannot suffice, that it is impossible to enforce a taste for a definite style where it is neither understood nor appreciated, and that taste must be gradually trained if a permanent result is to be achieved. Such were the views of the Holy Father often manifested in my presence.

But there was no narrowness in Pius X's conception of the sacred music that he considered acceptable. He by no means condemned local or national peculiarities, many of which he frankly admired, provided, he said, that the fundamental principles of maintaining their strictly religious character and gravity were scrupulously observed, if necessary, by means of careful adaptation. Nor did he wish to prohibit polyphonic music in church. He welcomed really good work by modern composers; nevertheless he required that it be invariably kept within the limits prescribed and constitute as it were an echo or development of plain chant. I remember his remarking that some enthusiasts wanted to go to extremes and banish from our churches all music that is not simply Gregorian chant: that he accounted to be an exaggerated fad. 'It would be the same,' he said, 'as if I were to discard the most beautiful and classical pictures of the Madonna, on the plea that the primitive and only acceptable type nowadays is the very earliest representation we possess of the Virgin Mother, such as we see it in the catacombs of St. Priscilla. We should thus be led to proscribe the masterpieces of ecclesiastical art and truly inspired paintings. We do not want profane pictures of our Lady, and the undevout images produced by many of our modern artists, but surely it would be unreasonable to assert that the most primitive pictures alone fulfil the conditions required by religion and by sound artistic taste. So it is with church music.'

One of his cherished wishes was to promote congregational singing wherever possible, for he held it to be most instructive for people of all classes and a powerful means of arousing an intelligent interest in the beauties of our sacred liturgy, especially in regard to the holy sacrifice of the Mass. He loved to dwell in this respect upon the remarkable results achieved in parishes where the congregation had been taught to sing correctly the different portions of the Mass in plain chant and the psalms and hymns at Sunday Vespers. He frequently expressed regret that more importance was not given to a practice which enabled people really to understand and deeply to feel the significance of Catholic worship, and which, if extensively applied, would attract so many to a knowledge and fulfilment of their religious duties. An effectual method of attaining this object appeared to him to be, that in every diocese a capable teacher of church music, approved by the Bishop, should spend a short time in each parish and there train a nucleus of singers, selected among the members of the congregation, who would soon lead the rest, and then go round again at intervals, to improve what he had initiated and encourage progress.

When musical compositions were presented for his acceptance, he carefully examined the score, and more than once I have heard him hum the melody which he read with perfect ease at first sight, marking time with his hand as he did so, and then giving his opinion upon the merits and style of the music.

Many have heard him sing Mass in St. Peter's or intone his solemn blessing in the Sistine Chapel and must recall his soft melodious voice.

## XI

## HIS CHARITY

At the close of each year, never later, to my recollection, than the following feast of the Epiphany, the Holy Father made a great point of auditing his private accounts, which he showed me on those occasions with evident pleasure. *'Presentiamo il bilancio al Segretario di Stato per il controllo,'* he used to say with a smile of satisfaction. He kept a ledger of the size of a thick copy-book, where on opposite pages he noted down day by day every sum he received, great or small, and every item of expenditure. The alms for Masses, that came to him from all parts of the world, he entered separately in a special book and over this register he was particularly scrupulous. 'I do not want to go to Purgatory for neglect in the matter of Masses,' was one of his customary remarks on this subject. But all other sums he set down in his one ledger, and when the year ran out he carefully subtracted from the total of free offerings the funds destined to special objects. Nothing could induce him to defer the distribution or modify the allotment of specific donations and he severely blamed the method too easily adopted by certain trustees of employing money contributed for a definite purpose, to provide for some urgent necessity or for supplying provisional aid in behalf of undertakings other than those intended by the donors, on the plea that the amount temporarily withdrawn could be replaced later on without detriment to those concerned.

I remember how after the terrible earthquake in Messina and Reggio Calabria, when very large sums had reached the Holy Father's hands for him to rebuild churches and schools and furnish relief to the destitute victims of the great catastrophe, not a few zealous people implored him to assign a portion of the Messina funds for other good works more or less connected with Sicily or Calabria. The Pope invariably refused their request. 'Not a penny,' he said, 'of what the faithful have given me for the victims of the earthquakes shall be spent on any other object however worthy of interest.

They have trusted me and I am responsible to them.'

And those funds, amounting to over six million francs, he administered and distributed himself personally. The balance sheet printed in the published account of all he accomplished in Sicily and Calabria is entirely his own, and he astonished the chief accountant at the Vatican by the rapidity and accuracy with which he ran up the endless lists of figures and jotted down the calculations necessary in dealing with the various sums required for different objects. When his financial report was issued, I recollect the following observation: 'I am wondering,' he said, 'whether perhaps this will not prove to be the only detailed report of the disposal of millions so generously contributed by the whole world for the relief of the stricken provinces.' He was not far wrong.

Pius X never stopped to haggle over what he gave away in charity, and he gave unceasingly; his impulse was to bestow all that he possessed. But not so in regard to himself: it was just the reverse, for then he enforced the strictest economy. On the day of his election to the Pontificate, or on the following morning, an enterprising jeweller had managed to proffer a very valuable pectoral cross and chain, in the hope of selling it to His Holiness.

Pius X wore it for several days, simply because he found it there among the new ornaments that he supposed himself called upon to adopt, and under the impression that this handsome cross and chain belonged to the papal treasury. Three weeks later, a bill for over three thousand francs came up for payment. 'Ah no,' the Holy Father immediately exclaimed, slowly shaking his head, 'you don't imagine, do you, that I am disposed to spend all this money on a cross for myself? Here, thank the man and return it at once. Surely there are plenty of crosses left by the late Pope, and in any case I shall be quite satisfied with the one I brought from Venice.' There and then he took off the new cross and it went back to the jeweller.

What difficulty one had to obtain leave to spend anything for his personal convenience, even in cases where his health was concerned. His medical adviser, Doctor Marchiafava, constantly insisted upon the necessity of his going out oftener to breathe fresh air; on the other hand he never ceased to complain of there being no other available access to the Vatican gardens except through the interminable and chilly galleries leading all round the Belvedere and the Library, through which the Holy Father had to pass before and after his outing, usually amidst the dust inevitably raised by throngs of sight-seers. The want of a private passage to the gardens had always been felt by his predecessor Leo XIII, though for him the inconvenience was lessened by the fact of his using habitually a sedan-chair. Pius X objected very much to being carried in this way, if for no other reason because the swinging movement made him giddy. After elaborate study and considerable discussion our architect at last solved the problem by finding it possible to pierce a tunnel which would connect the *Cortile del Belvedere* with the gardens and quite conveniently enable the Pope to drive there straight from the foot of his private lift or of the grand staircase of the palace. Nothing I could say however would persuade His Holi-

## HIS CHARITY

ness to undertake the expense of what appeared to him to be merely a personal comfort.

I finally succeeded in obtaining his consent to my having the tunnel built on my assuring him that I could procure the necessary money privately from friends, many of whom I knew would be glad and even proud to contribute to this improvement in the Vatican, especially when they realized the practical service they were rendering to him and to his successors. And so it proved to be.

## XII

## THE NEW CODE OF CANON LAW

THE reform of the Roman Curia, the foundation of the Biblical Institute, the building of central Seminaries and the legislation for the better training of the clergy, the new discipline regarding first and frequent Holy Communion, the restoration of church music, the powerful stand he made against the fatal errors of so-called Modernism, and the brave defence of the liberty of the Church in France, in Germany, in Portugal, in Russia and elsewhere, not to mention other acts of government, suffice indeed to single out Pius X as a great Pontiff and leader of men. I am in a position to testify that all this enormous work was due chiefly and often exclusively to his own personal initiative, and carefully thought out in his own mind. History will proclaim him a great deal more than merely a Pope whose 'goodness' nobody is inclined to question.

The limits I have set myself in tracing these brief memoirs forbid my entering upon a discussion of the various and important subjects I have just referred to, but one of his great undertakings deserves, I think, some special mention in keeping with the character of these sketches, *viz.* the New Code of Canon Law. Within the interval of a few days after his election he declared his definite intention of beginning the momentous enterprise which he had longed to see accomplished. Nor is it to be wondered at. Priest and Pastor he pre-eminently was, and by temperament a lover of practical and efficient measures; hence time and again he must have felt hampered in his administration by the network of successive legislation, of decrees that admitted various interpretations, of enactments that had grown obsolete or ill-suited to new conditions. A codification of Church Law appealed to him in the light of a measure full of promise for the maintenance of undying principles and likely to strengthen the vigour of ecclesiastical discipline, *Nova et Vetera*.

He cherished the hope of seeing this far-reaching reform introduced during his lifetime and at various stages of the preparatory studies I heard him exclaim: 'We must push on, for

I am growing old and I want to see the end.' God's Providence had disposed otherwise and after eleven years of unremitting labour that he watched over and directed at every step, he left an all but finished task to be crowned by his successor on the chair of Peter.

Benedict XV rendered a deserved and eloquent tribute to him when he promulgated the New Code. In a solemn Allocution to the Sacred College of Cardinals at the Consistory held on December 4, 1916, after summing up the reasons which had necessitated this revision of Church Law and the very great advantages which would ensue from its publication, the Pope went on to say: 'Divine Providence had ordained that the glory of rendering this immense service to the Church should fall to Pius X our predecessor of saintly memory. You are aware, Venerable Brethren, with what alacrity he set himself to this truly gigantic task at the very beginning of his pontificate, and with what seal and perseverance he pursued it during the whole time that he held the reins of government. And though it was not granted to him to complete his undertaking, nevertheless,

# THE NEW CODE OF CANON LAW

he alone must be accounted to be the author of the Code, and therefore will his name be handed down to posterity by the side of those Pontiffs of greatest fame in the annals of Canon Law, such as Innocent III, Honorious III and Gregory IX. For us it is enough to be able to promulgate that which he accomplished.'

As an illustration of the minuteness with which Pius X initiated the work of the New Code of Canon Law and directed the preparatory research, I cannot do better than reproduce here an autograph note of his which I have before me and which he handed to me on March 2, 1904.

The Holy Father wrote as follows: 'It will be well to decide immediately at the first meeting:

'I. In addition to Monsignor Gasparri (and also on his choice) to select two under-secretaries who can assist him in drawing up the reports of the meetings and substitute for him when he is unable to be present.

'II. To name the Rome Consultors.

'III. To select one or two Eminent Cardinals to preside over the congregations of Consultors.

'IV. To call upon the Bishops (*a*) to delegate one Consultor from among the Canonists of their respective districts, who shall come to Rome or draw up his judgement in writing; (*b*) to set forth the points of law upon which it appears suitable to make changes and to express their own opinions.

'V. To settle how often each month the Congregations of the Eminent Cardinals shall be held and how many times those of the Consultors.

'VI. Whether all the Consultors are to take up one Title of the Law simultaneously or whether it is preferable to distribute among them the matter that they are to discuss.

'VII. To recommend that the work should begin at once, without waiting for a more opportune time, because *dum Romæ consulitur Saguntum expugnatur*, and it is not suitable that, being as we are in Rome we should follow the Greek Kalends.'

# THE NEW CODE OF CANON LAW

Naturally whilst the work was proceeding it not infrequently occurred that opinions differed and it became difficult to decide upon the expediency of introducing some particular point of legislation or reform. Grave arguments would be marshalled for and against a given proposal. The views and desiderata of the Bishops in various parts of the world were not always in harmony and the Roman Consultors urged their reasons with sufficient force on both sides as to deserve serious consideration. Then it happened occasionally that Pius X, with that eminently practical instinct he so often manifested, would issue a decree in the direction which seemed to have the best support of valid arguments by way of experiment, to be eventually incorporated or not in the permanent legislation, thus allowing the possibility of correcting or even of withdrawing that particular enactment when the time came for drawing up the final text of the New Code. Failing to realize the wisdom of this procedure has led no doubt superficial observers to conclude rather hastily at times that Pius X or his successor Benedict XV had gone back upon definite decisions. Such is not the case. On the other hand it may be readily granted that there are perhaps some articles in the Code, as it stands today, which Pius X personally might have wished to frame otherwise, but he rarely forced his own preference in matters that were debatable and that did not imply the sacrifice of any essential principle.

## XIII

## HIS HUMILITY

*UBI humilitas ibi maiestas* (St. Augustine, Sermon 14). The truth of St. Augustine's axiom has been rarely, I think, so fully manifest as in the person of Pius X. Truly deep and unaffected humility was, I consider, the prominent characteristic of the Holy Father. It struck me to be so entirely the outstanding feature of his whole temperament as to have become in him a second nature. There was nothing in this of that shallow, cowed and false attitude of mind which is only indicative of weakness, or sometimes may be simply a form of self-consciousness, of a hidden craving for esteem or of a subtle dread of facing criticism. He was far too great a lover of truth and too sincerely genuine in everything to affect an outward appearance of virtue.

It cost him no effort to be humble, because he had a lowly conception of himself and the rooted conviction that we owe all our powers to God alone made it easier for him to admire the gifts he discerned in others rather than to discover any of them in himself.

Adulation or praise, in public or in private, was extremely repugnant to him, and if a person ventured to approach him in that way, he found either in a curt reply or in a playful remark the means of veiling his contempt. But, I confess that I fail to understand how anybody could attempt to flatter him, for even a spontaneous word of earnest admiration seemed to be out of place in his presence and to die away upon one's lips out of respect for the candour and dignity of his character. 'As silver is tried in the fining-pot and gold in the furnace, so a man is tried by the mouth of him that praiseth' (Prov. xxvii, 21).

He gave me the impression that in his private life it required a definite act on his part and almost a positive effort to realize that he was the Supreme Pontiff, endowed with all the prerogatives of that great office. Habitually, he appeared to consider himself the same humble priest of years gone by, or one of many bishops, without claim to special distinction. And yet, in the exercise of his sovereignty and leader-

## HIS HUMILITY

ship no one could have surpassed him in the stateliness of his demeanour or the vigour of his command.

Nevertheless, if I may hazard a comparison, it seemed natural to him to lay aside his eminent dignity and to assume it again when occasion arose, much in the same manner as he would put away or resume the tiara and robes that he had to wear during the solemn ceremonies he performed so majestically in the Sistine Chapel or in St. Peter's.

As an instance of what I am trying to describe, I may recall an incident that more particularly drew my attention in two different cases. I happened to be laying before the Holy Father a bishop's urgent request for an exceptional faculty in circumstances that demanded the direct intervention of His Holiness. After listening attentively to my report, he slowly read over the document himself, and then, without raising his eyes, said: 'This is a faculty which the Pope alone can grant.' 'Yes, Holy Father,' I replied, 'and that is why I have come to trouble you about it.' Whereupon, quite seriously, almost under his breath, and as if communing with himself, he added: 'No doubt, no doubt, let us act as Pope' (*Gia, gia, facciamo da Papa*). And taking up his pen he wrote out the dispensation in due form, and handing it back to me, passed on to discuss other matters.

A similar trend of thought revealed itself sometimes in a word that rose to his lips in presence of unsought tokens of respect which he could not avoid. Quite recently the Bishop of Angers was describing to me the indelible impressions of his first audience with His Holiness. 'I was on my knees,' relates Monsignor Rumeau, 'at the feet of Pius X, but my attitude visibly distressed him and bidding me to rise at once, he protested, saying: "No; not on your knees, Monsignor, for I am the last of God's priests!" (*Io sono l'ultimo dei sacerdoti di Dio*). And when I pressed him for advice upon a grave matter, I noticed that before replying he invariably turned his eyes to the crucifix on his table, as if seeking counsel there.'

*Ubi humilitas ibi maiestas.* Simple as were his habits, fatherly and homely as he appeared in private, the dignity of his countenance, the quiet unassuming nobility of his whole bearing, never failed to impress all those who attended his official receptions or had the privilege of seeing him officiate on great occasions. How many I have met who lay claim to high lineage and exalted birth who might have learnt from Pius X a distinction which they lacked.

Nor did his sentiments belie his outward demeanour. The delicacy of his feelings showed forth at every step, so true is it that refinement may just as often be the result of virtue as the merely accidental product of high descent. I have already spoken of his exquisite regard for others; I may add that one of the things most repugnant to him and which roused his indignation was that his servants should be blamed for acts that were not their own or be censured for failures in which they had incurred no personal responsibility. To speak only of my own experience; it is of course inevitable that a Cardinal Secretary of State should have to run the gauntlet of criticism from many quarters, both in public and in private. He must be ready to bear the brunt of undeserved abuse for the mistakes of others and to be saddled indiscriminately with the authorship of acts that are not always his and of which he may not have had control. That is all in his day's work. But its recurrence caused real pain to Pius X and at times gave rise to his indignant protest. 'I cannot stand such injustice,' he would exclaim. 'Let them inveigh against me, if they please. If anybody is at fault, it is I. Why should you always be blamed for everything?' And what he thus felt in regard to me, he felt no less in respect to other officials, not excluding those whose position was the humblest. He never sought cover behind those who served him.

Not infrequently I found it very difficult to persuade him to let us face the outcry, as in duty bound, and stand between him and his opponents, even in cases in which we were not directly responsible. But this went against the grain and distressed him, because it struck him as unworthy and unfair. In addition, when disapproving the acts of his subordinates and suffering by their blunders, he strove to excuse and cover their mistakes.

Not many people, I fancy, had occasion to realize fully how gifted the Holy Father was or to appreciate the wide extent of his attainments, for the very simple reason that he made a point of concealing them whenever possible; he failed to do so however when thrown off his guard, especially in the presence of those who lived in his intimacy. He delighted in seeing others win credit for success entirely due to his suggestions and for work that was all his own. Sometimes when their praises were sung without any mention of his name, he would look intensely amused and afterwards say to me with a humorous smile: 'I think I too had a share in that.'

In letters to me, and also to other advisers whose counsel he sought regarding a plan he had conceived or the tenor of a document he had himself prepared, he constantly concluded with the express injunction that we were to correct, suppress or add whatever we thought fit. In cases in which his own scheme met with disapproval, he welcomed reasonable criticism from any quarter without the slightest sign of annoyance, and if convinced, I have often heard him remark: 'Well, my work has come to nothing. No doubt there are wiser heads than mine. I dare say they know best.' Though it not rarely happened that his original idea turned out eventually to be correct and should have been preferred, he avoided dwelling upon the mistake committed and strove to shield those responsible from blame and criticism.

Nothing could induce Pius X to exalt his own family, nor did he ever dream of raising the social position of his relatives in view of the high office to which he himself had been called. 'When I die,' he used to say, 'my sisters will go back to their knitting. They shall have the benefit of my life-insurance.' Let me add at once, that I never knew anyone of his numerous relations to express the slightest regret at his attitude in this respect. They all, beginning with his own brother, took it as a matter of course.

We were well aware of the warm affection he entertained for his nephew, Monsignor Giovanni Battista Parolin, a priest whose high character had won unstinted esteem on all sides. Quite naturally therefore most people expected the Holy Father to employ his services in the Vatican and thus have the pleasure of his attendance and company. There can be no doubt

## HIS HUMILITY

that an arrangement of this kind would have afforded His Holiness very real gratification and that the presence of Monsignor Parolin in his intimate life would have procured him relief from the tedious formality of his official duties. But our repeated efforts to persuade him to allow himself a legitimate satisfaction that nobody could possibly find fault with, inevitably failed. His answer always was: 'Yes, Don Battista is a good priest, but he is young and he must work in the ministry. He has a parish and he is better there than in a palace.' In 1913, Monsignor Parolin, after ten years of strenuous work in the parish of Possagno, up on the hills, was promoted by his Bishop, Monsignor Longhin, to a canonry and placed in charge of the Cathedral parish at Treviso. He found the presbytery there in a most dilapidated condition and in need of urgent repairs. Pius X came to the rescue and restored the building upon which he spent twenty-five thousand lire. On handing the sum to his nephew, the Pope said in his characteristic way: 'There, this is my present for your promotion; you must not expect anything more from me.' It was the next Pope,

Benedict XV, who, at my proposal, on the very day of his election, named Monsignor Parolin a Canon of St. Peter's.

Monsignor Parolin only came to Rome on a ten days' visit, twice or three times each year. On one occasion, whilst conversing with His Holiness during the hot hours of a midsummer's afternoon, the Holy Father felt very thirsty and would have liked a glass of water. Monsignor Parolin naturally rose up at once to ring for a servant; but the Holy Father checked him, because, he said, his private attendant had gone out and perhaps might feel hurt if on his return he appeared to have neglected his duty and found that another had taken his place. So he went without his glass of water until supper time.

In the same spirit of detachment and on the principle of emphasizing a clear distinction between his own person, of which he thought so little, and the privileges of his exalted rank, which he could not ignore, he never consented to allow his sisters a residence in the Vatican, though so many others lived there who were far less entitled to the favour. He provided them

# HIS HUMILITY

with a small apartment in the neighbouring Piazza and received their visit once or twice a week, usually on Wednesdays and Sundays. Though he made no reference to the matter, I feel sure that the line he took cost him a real sacrifice, for his sisters, so devoted to him, were worthy indeed of the affection he entertained for them. When Rosa, the eldest, to whom he was particularly attached, fell ill and died, the privation of not being able to attend her at the last weighed heavily upon him. No less in keeping with this attitude regarding himself and all that concerned him personally, in his last Will he did not go beyond expressing the request that a sum of one hundred lire a month should be granted to three of his sisters then living in Rome. A strange contrast indeed with the regal generosity he showed whenever an opportunity offered of assisting those in need.

The precise clauses of the last Will and Testament of Pius X in regard to his family, are as follows:

'Born poor, having lived poor and certain to die very poor, I regret being unable to repay the many persons who have rendered me special service, particularly in Mantua, in Venice and in Rome, and therefore since I cannot give them any other sign of gratitude, I pray God to reward them with his choicest blessings. Having to provide for my sisters, Rosa, Maria and Anna, who have always lived with me and served me without the slightest remuneration, I recommend them to the generosity of the Holy See, that so long as one of them lives a monthly allowance of three hundred lire be allotted to them. All my other near blood relations being poor, I pray the Holy See to grant one thousand lire a year, during their lifetime, to my brother Angelo Sarto and to my other sisters Teresa, Antonia and Lucia. . . . The premium of ten thousand lire to be paid by the Life Insurance Company, shall be divided in equal shares between my brother and my sisters.' (June 12, 1911.)

# XIV

## LAST ILLNESS AND DEATH

'Well done, good and faithful servant!'
—Matt. xxv.

How suddenly the end came! After the attack of influenza which the Holy Father underwent in 1913, due undoubtedly in great measure to his having overworked himself, Pius X recovered his strength in a most remarkable way. In truth he was never as ill as people were led to believe at the time by exaggerated reports in the daily press, and he was so cheerful and full of life all through his sickness and convalescence that it proved difficult to prevail upon him to lie idle.

'Were it not for these worthy doctors, and could I have my own way, I should be up and about long since,' is what he cheerily repeated during the days he spent in bed. Often did I see him start up energetically from his pillow to sign a document that I presented to him and exclaim with a smile and his hand firmly extended: 'Eminence, you see my hand does not shake,' and thereupon proceed to append his signature with his habitual energy.

On his return to his usual life he seemed to be very much better in health than I had seen him for many a year. His activity increased. He appeared to have acquired renewed vigour and almost to have thrown off something of the burden of age. The enforced rest had been obviously a blessing in disguise and there was every reason for supposing that he would be spared for several years ahead.

And so did he continue until August, 1914, up to the outbreak of the Great War. How deeply he was affected by the fearful tragedy it is difficult to say. As I have already related, he had long foreseen and explicitly foretold the advent of the European conflict. The horror and pain that overwhelmed him when it actually broke out was intense. Day and night the awful spectacle of the appalling struggle haunted his mind together with the forecast of all the suffering and anguish that must inevitably follow in its train.

## LAST ILLNESS AND DEATH

The invasion of Belgium and the news of the first battles filled him with the bitterest grief. He feverishly awaited the documentary evidence of all the facts in order to trace his definite line of action and to enable him to raise his fearless voice in the defence of the sacred principles of justice and of peace. The Master's call came before he had time to do more than issue a preliminary exhortation which bears the date of August 2.

After the feast of the Assumption, August 15, the Holy Father showed signs of a slight catarrhal indisposition; but neither he himself nor those in attendance attributed importance to a trifling disorder apparently due chiefly if not exclusively to the excessive heat of a trying summer. I myself was somewhat poorly, and on Tuesday, August 18, feeling unable to go up that morning to despatch business with the Holy Father, I deputed Monsignor Canali, the *Sostituto* of the Secretariate, to submit to His Holiness one or two more urgent matters I had in hand. He returned with the report that the Pope did not reveal any symptoms of sickness and a personal message from him that there was nothing much amiss. 'Tell the Cardinal,' were his words, 'to get well, for when he is ill I am ill, too.' His doctors, ever watchful and inclined to take no risks, made light of his indisposition and after prescribing a very ordinary remedy expressed their conviction that a day would suffice to set him right. His sisters, usually over-anxious whenever they detected the smallest sign of an ailment, were not in the least disturbed at this stage. They went out of their way to let me know that there was nothing to worry about and that I should find the Holy Father quite well the next morning.

No one has been able to account for the sudden change that occurred during the following night. Monsignor Bressan, the Pope's devoted chaplain, who slept in an adjoining room and within hearing, only noticed that the Holy Father was rather restless and nothing more. However, as he failed to rise at the usual hour, Monsignor Bressan went to him and found him feverish and in pain. The doctors were immediately summoned. On examination they discovered that the Holy Father's lungs were congested and they pronounced

## LAST ILLNESS AND DEATH

him to be very seriously ill. About eight o'clock they came down to give me this news. Their report fairly staggered me, for I realized at once the full gravity of the case and the danger of heart failure. I told Doctor Marchiafava that I considered that the end was at hand. In my opinion the Holy Father was suffering far too much under the strain of impressions caused by public events to offer prolonged resistance in the face of serious illness. Though inclined to think me somewhat pessimistic, the doctors diagnosed the case as exceedingly grave but not desperate and still withheld their final verdict.

The announcement that Pius X lay dangerously ill spread quickly throughout the town and people of all classes flocked to the Vatican for news. Many who only a few days since had seen him in excellent health could not bring themselves to believe that he was dying. At ten o'clock a severe crisis ensued. I hurried to the Holy Father's bedside and found him gasping for breath. The doctors had been called back and were applying every possible remedy, with the assistance of a Brother of St. John of God. The moment he saw me he clasped my hand firmly. 'Eminenza! . . . Eminenza! . . .' was all he said. The imminent danger of a fatal collapse made it imperative to give him the Sacraments without further delay. The last consecutive words I heard from his lips were: 'I resign myself completely.' Shortly after that he lost all power of speech, though perfectly conscious, and looking intelligently from one to the other he manifested beyond doubt that he realized his condition.

The Holy Viaticum and Extreme Unction were administered to him by Monsignor Sacrista in the simplest form possible. On a little table by the bedside, covered with a white cloth, a crucifix and two lighted candles were the only evidence of ceremony. I could not help thinking that after all Pius X was receiving the last rites of the Church in the way most congenial to him and that he must be glad to avoid the publicity and solemnity which usually surround the death-bed of a Pontiff. It was not unlike the scene one might have witnessed in the humblest cottage of a dying labourer, without pomp or splendour of any kind. His devoted sisters stood by in tearful silence; but we were very few, owing to the suddenness of all that had happened. Very graphically has this moment been described in the following words: 'One was not conscious of time and it was all unreal. Suddenly the deep notes of St. Peter's great bell boomed out, tolling *pro Pontifice agonizante*, and at that signal Exposition of the Blessed Sacrament began in all the patriarchal Basilicas with special prayers. The hot sirocco, the buzz from the Piazza San Pietro far below, whispering prelates and attendants, the boom of the bell, how strange it all seemed; and behind everything the catastrophe of the present public situation and war.'

There is no ground for the statement made occasionally that during the preceding weeks the Holy Father's health had caused us anxiety, and in support of what I have already said in this respect I may add that most of the cardinals were away from Rome for their summer vacation. Indeed had it not been for the outbreak of the war, I myself should have gone to Monte Mario, at a short distance from the Vatican, as the Pope so kindly urged upon me to do each year, after the anniversary of his coronation on August 9.

We lost no time in informing the few cardinals still in residence of His Holiness' precarious condition and they hastened to the Palace in great anxiety, the first to come being Cardinal Bisleti. Telegrams were despatched from the Secretariate of State to the members of the Sacred College, and Cardinal Della Volpe, the Camerlengo, arrived in Rome the following morning.

The energetic measures adopted by the doctors produced their result and the Holy Father rallied considerably. All through the day he remained half sitting, propped up with pillows, perfectly calm and peaceful. No further crisis occurred to disturb the serenity of his countenance; no gesture of agitation or complaint ever escaped him. Though unable to speak, he recognized those around him and from time to time he slowly made the sign of the cross. The long summer day wore on interminably whilst we sat in the adjoining room within sight of his bed, in order to leave him as much air as pos-

## LAST ILLNESS AND DEATH

sible, and we watched through the seemingly endless hours for his passage to eternity.

About eleven at night, I stepped into his room, noiselessly I thought, from the opposite side to the one towards which he was reclining. But he immediately turned his head and his piercing look followed me whilst I went slowly round the foot of the bed. As I approached he raised an arm to welcome me and when I sat down quite near to him, he seized my hand and held it in his grasp with a vigour that astonished me. He then gazed intently at me and his eyes were riveted on mine. How I longed to read his thoughts at that moment and to hear his voice whilst we looked so steadfastly at each other! What was it he was endeavouring to convey in those eyes that seemed to speak? Was he recalling the long years I had spent in familiar intercourse with him and all we had endured together? Was he trying to comfort me with a last message in the grief I strove in vain to conceal?

He held me thus motionless for nearly forty minutes. From time to time he loosened his grasp to caress me and then again took up my hand in his.

At last he let his head sink back wearily upon the pillow and his eyes closed. He seemed to have bidden me farewell. Never shall I forget the scene of our parting. It is as vividly before me now as it was on that memorable night, when I found myself repeating the words of St. Lawrence which we had read in the Breviary a few days previously: *Quo progrederis sine filio, pater? quo sacerdos sancte sine ministro properas?*

Shortly afterwards Doctor Marchiafava, who was in the next room, writing out the last official bulletin of the Pope's condition, beckoned me to his side, and to my surprise requested me to assist him in drawing up the text. On my asking him how I could possibly be of the slightest use in a matter regarding which I was obviously incompetent, the doctor replied that I had mistaken his meaning; he did not call upon me to assist him in framing the technical report, but merely to suggest a word that would give an idea at all events of the extraordinary serenity of the Holy Father's attitude in the face

## LAST ILLNESS AND DEATH

of death. 'Look at him,' he said, 'is he not truly wonderful?'

Towards midnight I was prevailed upon to go and rest awhile, being assured that His Holiness would still live on for several hours. An hour later a message came for me to hurry back, but before I could reach his bedside Pius X had gently passed away and his beautiful soul was with God.

## XV

## HIS RELATIVES

BEFORE bringing these sketches to a close, I should like to place on record some facts concerning the family of Pius X, which have come more particularly to my personal knowledge, for they illustrate the domestic traditions of his home and throw light upon the environment which had helped to shape his individual character and which he had further emphasized by his own virtues. I have already referred to the self-denial that led him to refrain from seeking temporal advantages for his own relations, as he might so easily have done in the various stages of his exalted career.

In this he gave the world at large, and the clergy in particular, an almost unparalleled example of his disinterestedness and of his singleness of mind in the pursuit of his lofty spiritual aims.

When the disastrous invasion of the Venetian provinces took place in the autumn of 1917, and the enemy swept across the land between the Isonzo and the Piave, it became necessary to evacuate with all haste the towns and villages that lay within the line of battle, either to avoid falling into the hands of the invaders, or in order to facilitate the urgent task of immediate defence. The people fled by thousands and among the hapless refugees from Gemona, Cavaso, Venice, Saizano, Riese and every other district, there were many nephews and nieces of Pius X.

None of them had ever lived in wealth. They earned a modest living in different ways and they were not destitute. One was a sculptor, two or three held positions as school teachers; some again conducted a small trade or had secured employment in a local administration.

When the storm burst, twenty-three of them, men, women, and children, were constrained to fly in a few hours, and, forsaking their quiet homes and belongings, with no more luggage than a small bundle each, several of their number started off on foot, trudging along for miles in quest of a railway that would convey them to some temporary refuge. Giuseppina Parolin Salvadori, one of the Pope's nieces, escaped with difficulty from Gemona, under fire; she went through untold suffering, alone and unprotected, for she was separated from her husband in her flight across the Tagliamento.

After an endless journey, the dreadful discomfort of which I need not stop to describe, they all reached Rome one night and made their way to the small apartment in Piazza Rusticucci, where the late Pope's sisters were living. Hospitality was not refused them; it was a matter of course, though the most indispensable means of providing there and then for twenty-three unexpected visitors were not forthcoming. No rooms, no beds and few of the necessaries of life. Huddled together during that first night and the following day, they were indeed to be pitied; and they were the Holy Father's relations!

I went to meet them as soon as possible, in the hope of being able to lend some help. The scene I witnessed will ever remain vividly impressed upon my memory. I found them assembled in one room, where they sat in a circle or stood, for there were not chairs sufficient

## HIS RELATIVES

for all. I saw children of different ages; two or three tiny ones nestled in their mothers' arms or rested on their fathers' knees, whilst other older ones looked on with wondering eyes. All present appeared quite resigned and self controlled. I heard no lamentations; nobody made a display of sentiment, though their haggard faces revealed only too clearly the great hardships they had undergone. Their whole attitude was full of dignity and admirably simple, the same that one always discerned in Pius X.

They replied to my questions in a few words and my assurance of sympathy only drew forth the remark that 'there were so many other poor people suffering as much or more than they had had to endure.' When I urged them to tell me what provision they most needed, the answer invariably was: 'We should like to find work, in order not to be a burden to others; if your Eminence can assist us in this way, we shall be deeply grateful.'

But that which impressed me more than aught else was, that neither then, nor later on, nor at any time, did a single one of them ever mention or even in directly refer to their close relationship with the late Pontiff, nor appear to consider that this exceptional circumstance gave them any title for special consideration in the eyes of others or afforded the least claim upon the generosity of the Holy See. This point of view did not seem to have entered their minds. Benedict XV, to whom I spoke of this rare and edifying example, fully shared my admiration and all the more willingly did he contribute to the relief of such noble sufferers.

I experienced little difficulty in finding temporary employment for them, because every request in their favour met with cordial sympathy. The Jesuit Fathers at the Collegio Massimo gladly accepted the services of one of them as a teacher; two others were soon engaged as private clerks, and the Sisters of the *Doctrine Chrétienne* welcomed Signora I. Parolin, a schoolmistress, who took charge of a girls' class in their school on Monteverde.

The Spanish Embassy kindly gave lodging to one batch of refugees in the hostel attached to the National Church, in via Monserrato, and the Augustinian Fathers at Santa Monica offered generous hospitality to another group.

The Franciscan Missionaries of Mary who had Care of the Institute founded by Pius X, on the via Portuense, for the poor orphans from Messina and Reggio Calabria, were only too delighted to provide a refuge for three little nieces of the beloved founder. Most assuredly, Pius X never imagined that the home he had so munificently supplied for the victims of the great earthquake, would one day open its doors to his own kith and kin, victims of the Great War.

Lastly I may mention the case of Bepi Vigna, a boy of fourteen, whose father worked in the arsenal at Venice, and who himself was an apprentice there. We managed to get him admitted into a factory at some distance behind St. Peter's. Every morning he passed under my windows on his way to work, clad in a simple blouse, and he earned two lire a day! Not a very remunerative occupation, it may be said, nor a very distinguished position for one who only three years previously would have met with special regard at the Vatican, as one related to the reigning Pontiff. But neither he nor his family stopped to consider this, and his employers, a month later, whilst testifying to his good behaviour, expressed their astonishment that he had never mentioned to his companions nor to anybody at the factory that he was a great-nephew of Pius X.

Immediately after the signing of the armistice, all these exemplary refugees hurried back to their homes, but alas! under trying conditions and very different circumstances to those they had known before the war.